KU-165-671

WITHDRAWN FROM
THE NEELB LIBRARY SERVICE
ON ....
FOR SALE AT

FLYFISHING
- Tactics on small streams

FLYFISHING
–Tactics on small streams

LOU STEVENS

NORTH EASTERN LIBRARY SERVICE
AREA LIBRARY. DEMESNE AVENUE
BALLYMENA, CO ANTRIM BT43 7BG

NUMBER   4511309

CLASS   799.12

BLANDFORD PRESS
LONDON · NEW YORK · SYDNEY

First published in the UK 1988 by Blandford Press, an imprint of Cassell plc,
Artillery House, Artillery Row, London SW1P 1RT

Copyright © Lou Stevens 1988

Distributed in the United States by
Sterling Publishing Co, Inc,
2 Park Avenue, New York, NY 10016

Distributed in Australia by
Capricorn Link (Australia) Pty Ltd
PO Box 665, Lane Cove, NSW 2066

British Library Cataloguing in Publication Data

Stevens, Lou
Flyfishing: tactics on small streams.
1. Fly fishing
I. Title
799.1'2

ISBN 0-7137-2040-9

All rights reserved.
No part of this book may be reproduced
or transmitted in any form or by any means,
electronic or mechanical, including photocopying,
recording or any information storage and
retrieval system, without permission
in writing from the Publisher.

Typeset at the Alden Press Oxford London and Northampton

Printed in the U.K. by Biddles Ltd., Guildford

To my wife, Kay,
her endless patience has enabled me
to pursue my obsession with trout.

CONTENTS

INTRODUCTION

The sport of flyfishing is blessed with an abundance of rich literature. Many of the early works are now considered classics and are still avidly read today. The wisdoms and truths they contain are as applicable now as the day they were written.

The advent of the stocked reservoir opened up the sport to literally millions of troutfishermen, and literature on the art and craft of still-water fishing became prolific. Not all of what was written was good, but it filled a void as most previously available literature dealt with river fishing, with a decided emphasis on the chalk stream. The good literature on still-water troutfishing will take its place alongside the early classics, and will be referred to for many years to come.

However, it is a sad fact that many of the new flyfishers have never known the joy of fishing a trout stream. Chalk streams are not available to them, and the 'wild brownie' of the small stream remains a mystery.

Still-water angling literature, although so very important to the sport, has not helped this situation. Reservoir fishing has become a branch of flyfishing in its own right and its devotees have become still-water specialists. The small stream has become neglected. For the first time in many years permission to fish is often easy to obtain and the wild, stream-bred brownie is available to all.

I

It is my hope that the following pages will induce some of my fellow anglers to consider these small streams and to savour the joy that can be had in pursuit of the wild brownie.

Lou Stevens

CHAPTER 1

THE WATER

A brook, a beck, a moorland stream or a burn – call it what you will – is the type of water I hope, in these pages, we will fish together. It is the harsh, exciting world of the wild brownie. Perhaps its source is high in the hills from ice-cold springs, from where it cascades from one rocky pool to another down a densely-wooded valley. At times it may be barely visible through the thick growth along its banks and through the overhanging branches that form a canopy over the water.

It is also possible that it had its start in life in some remote moorland bog, and now it gurgles its way between barren hills and crags exposed to all the elements, yet growing stronger and stronger as it gathers water from that rugged environment.

These are not serene chalk streams. There is no lush, aquatic plant-life thriving in alkaline water with an abundance of underwater insect activity. In our type of stream the scant plant-life struggles to find a foothold in the stony bed, and loses that slender hold during the spate that follows every heavy rainfall. Our trout will not be fat and gorged: our trout will be strong, wild brownies who from their birth have had to fight the elements, to fight for every morsel of food, and – for their very survival – to learn how to avoid their enemies.

1

An over-grown stream in the English midlands. This type of water especially should not be overlooked – large brownies often make their home in such apparently unpromising streams

You will need all your ingenuity to overcome the many and varied problems these streams present. In reality we are not just fishing a stream, we are fishing a variety of different waters along each short stretch. Water flow will be fast in one place, slow in another. The depth will vary from very deep to barely enough to cover the stones – and all within a few paces.

The sparse, aquatic plant-life is often taken to indicate a complete lack of underwater insects. This is, however, not necessarily the case. True, aquatic fly-nymphs are not so numerous as they might be but they are there in fair number. In fact, some small streams have very good and very regular hatches. It must also be remembered that there are many other forms of underwater life besides nymphs.

Our wild brownie is an expert at finding food – he has to

2

The River Towy, Dyfed. Note the angler in
the distance fishing off the exposed rocks. It would have
been better if he had chosen the opposite bank, and taken
advantage of the cover

be to survive. However, the perils he faces in the small stream
have made him very wary, much more wary than his fat
cousin in better waters. He is often hungry and eager for
food, but his instinct for survival comes first.

Very few flyfishers give this type of water the attention it
deserves. Perhaps under the impression that all the trout will
be far too small, they pass up any opportunity to fish these
waters in favour of the local reservoir and its stocked
rainbows. I feel this to be a sad state of affairs. The fish in our
small streams may not be huge – perhaps averaging only two
or three to the pound – but they are wild, stream-bred fish,
lively and beautifully coloured. They will put up a terrific
fight on the ultra-light tackle we have to use to outwit them
and, of course, there is always the chance of the stream
monster. It is always a source of amazement to me that large

trout – over $1\frac{1}{2}$ lb (0.7 kg) – are often found in the most unlikely places, sometimes in water barely deep enough to cover them.

This type of fishing also enables us to revitalise our flyfishing skills: we won't catch wild brownies in a small stream by casting a size-6 lure tied on a 6 lb (2.7 kg) tippet. This is not meant to decry reservoir fishing with its special techniques. On the contrary, some of our most respected and skilful flyfishers have specialised to the extent that reservoir fishing may now be considered a separate branch of flyfishing. However, I do advance the theory that going back to basics – using ultra-light tackle and reading a stream yard by yard – never hurt any serious flyfisher. It will improve their casting, reactions, and perhaps their knowledge and understanding of trout.

Permission to fish these small streams is usually easy to obtain. Very often a local club has the fishing rights, and day or season tickets are readily available at quite reasonable prices. It must be remembered that many small streams have sea-trout and salmon runs, and your acceptance on the water may well depend on your making it very clear that you only intend to fish for native trout. In many such cases the locals have little interest in native trout, and you will find at times that you have the stream to yourself.

As mentioned at the beginning of this chapter, through these pages we will fish the small stream together. We will talk as we go but it may well be a one-sided conversation. That is regretted, but let us hope that we both gain much pleasure from it.

So, let's go fishing for wild brownies with a fly – but first, it's necessary to discuss the tackle we will use.

CHAPTER 2

TACKLE

Whatever is said about tackle there will always be someone to disagree. This is as it should be, for what is right for one person may not necessarily suit another. Basically it could be argued that everyone uses whatever suits them best – or is best suited to their particular type of fishing. In reality, however, it only sometimes works out that way.

Many anglers buy a rod that is completely unsuited to themselves and to the type of fishing they intend to do. Then, over a period of time, they adjust themselves to suit the rod. The result is that they never attain the degree of casting skill they envy in others, and many of the joys of flyfishing are permanently lost to them. Others, over the years, collect several rods and end up using one in particular, which they refer to as their favourite, not realising that the so-called favourite is, in fact, the right rod both for them and the type of fishing they do.

My own favourite rod is a 5 ft (1.5 m) wand of one-piece split-cane, weighing only $1\frac{5}{8}$ oz (46 g) – certainly not a rod I would suggest is right for everyone, nor necessarily right for general stream fishing. I only mention it here to show my personal preference for ultra-light tackle when fishing a small stream.

My recommendation would be for a rod not exceeding

$7\frac{1}{2}$ ft (2.3 m). Longer rods are an abomination on a small and possibly over-grown water. Side-casting is normal practice on small streams in order to miss overhead branches, and side-casting with a rod over $7\frac{1}{2}$ ft (2.3 m) in length invariably results in real trouble with over-grown banks. A short rod will do all we require – even a decent roll-cast as long as we are not too ambitious as to the length of cast. However, you will find that nearly all our casting will be short length – 10–18 yd (9–16.5 m).

The question as to the best material for the rod is a difficult one for we all have our preferences – not always formed from sound facts. A short rod needs to be considered in relation to its size. By this I mean the material from which it is made needs to be of light weight so that the casting action is not impaired. A short rod is invariably made with a fast action (what might be described as a 'dry-fly' action), otherwise casting with so short a length would be extremely difficult. This fast action has another advantage: it enables us to use a flyline of reasonable weight, say a no. 4, 5 or 6. So I would not, personally, be bothered if the rod was of split-cane, carbon, or glass fibre – provided it had a good, fast action, was light in weight, and handled a reasonable weight line. Perhaps split-cane will give better service over the years. Carbon and glass-fibre rods are much more fragile than you think, but with reasonable care all three materials are quite suitable.

The fittings on a rod are important. If you have the choice, stay away from the new, rubber-composition handgrips – they may be very good on large flyrods or sea-fishing rods but they have no place on a rod of the size we are talking about. A small rod has, by necessity, a small handgrip surface, and for a sure grip I know of nothing that equals cork.

The reel-seat should be of the two-ring type, either two sliding rings or a sliding ring and fixed butt-cap (see Fig. 1).

6

Fig. 1 An ideal reel-seat for a short rod

Note A sliding ring and butt-cap have the advantage of securing the reel at the very end of the rod – a great aid to casting

7

This will keep the weight to a minimum and at the same time leave as much handgrip available as possible. This weight business is most important if a short rod is not to feel butt-heavy – remember, we have yet to add a reel and a line, all making for additional weight. The reel itself is of limited importance. I do not agree with the theory that reels balance rods: I believe that a reel should not interfere with the rod action in any way. A reel that makes a rod feel butt-heavy is too big or heavy for that particular rod. The reverse is also true. So, when considering the reel we are really concerned with two things: first, will it be light enough in view of the small rod we are using; and second, will it hold sufficient line?

Let us think a little about line capacity. If, say, our rod takes a no. 5 line, we do not necessarily need a reel that will hold a full-length double-taper no. 5 line plus backing. On a small stream we rarely use more than 20 yd (18.3 m) of flyline in actual fishing, and we are not being very practical if we insist on yards and yards of backing. Let's face it, even a good-size fish has little chance of running far in a small stream. In fact, he won't try, he'll endeavour to free himself by short runs and hard tugging – and if that fails he'll head for the snags!

So I would advocate cutting a flyline down to a 20-yd (18.3-m) length, then carefully needle-knotting on a length of fine line-backing – say, another 20 yd (18.3 m). This approach allows us to use a much smaller reel that will not upset the action of our shorter rod and, equally important, we reduce the weight of the rod at the butt end.

While on the subject of flylines, I would like to mention the portion at the end of the taper – the working end. Most manufacturers make their lines with the taper ending in a level portion of some 24 in (0.6 m). This is an ideal design for general flyfishing where leaders may vary from $7\frac{1}{2}$ ft (2.3 m) to 18 ft (5.5 m). I am going to recommend, however, that we use a different leader system – more about that later. In the meantime, I am going to make the suggestion that this level portion of flyline be reduced by 6 to 8 in (152 to 203 mm). We won't discuss it any further at this stage. I just ask you to remember the point. The time will come when you are fishing with a short rod, casting a short line, and the cast will not be as delicate as you would wish – this is then the time to remember and think about that 6 to 8 in (152 to 203 mm). Still on the subject of flylines, don't be tempted to use a weight-forward line. These lines were designed for long-distance casting, which is neither necessary nor desirable on a small stream. Consequently, they are not only of no help to us but also they make a good roll-cast almost an impossibility. A double-taper line is the best choice.

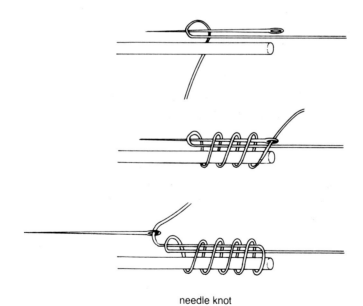

needle knot

Fig. 2A Needle-knot

The best knot for joining the tippet to the braided leader

9

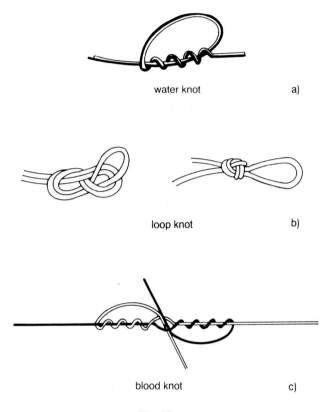

water knot   a)

loop knot   b)

blood knot   c)

Fig. 2B

(a) Water-knot An alternative to the needle-knot – but not as neat or secure
(b) Loop-knot A secure knot to form the small loop to take the fine tippet
extension
(c) Blood-knot Useful knot for joining the fine tippet to the leader loop – also
for attaching fly to tippet

Flylines today are made in so many grades – floating, fast-sinking, slow-sinking, sink-tip, intermediate – the list grows every year. All have their uses, sometimes specialist uses, and the growth in reservoir fishing has been responsible for much of the research that has taken place. In our case, rarely fishing water over 10 ft (3 m) deep, a floating line has to be our first choice. By using a sinkant on our leaders we are able to reach most of the depths we are likely to encounter. However, a sink-tip line is a useful accessory in the spring or during spate conditions, and such a line on a spare spool takes up little room in a fishing bag.

Now let's talk about the working end of the equipment – the leader. For years I was unhappy with the knotless, tapered leader as sold by the tackle shops. This type of leader, if it is fine enough at the tippet end, is never heavy enough at the butt end. Adding a thicker strand of nylon to the butt, of possibly a completely different quality, does very little to improve matters. Then there is the problem of the ever-disappearing tippet as one changes flies. Oh, yes, I know one can add a further length of tippet from time to time, but that brings up the same problem as adding to the butt end – it destroys the taper.

So, I made up my own leaders, blood-knotting lengths of nylon together and designing different tapers, all very fine except for the problem of straightening them out! I soon found that no matter how hard one tried to straighten out a knotted leader there were always kinks at the blood-knots that couldn't be reached with that useful bit of rubber.

We are fortunate today that there is a ready-made answer to the problem: I'm talking about the fairly-new, braided, tapered leader. This type of leader has a good, heavy butt end, it never needs straightening as it has no kinks or coils, and it can be made to float or to sink, just as you wish. However, I am not satisfied that it has yet attained the perfect design, and I am certain we can improve on it.

If you look at Fig. 3 you will readily see what I suggest. The reason for the 12-in (0.3-m) length of 3 × nylon before the tippet is not to improve the taper, it is to overcome the problems caused by snags. Everything will break at its weakest point, and the weakest point of a braided leader is

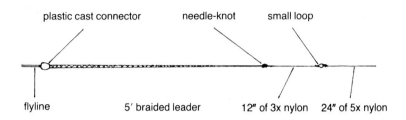

Fig. 3 The leader

usually at the needle-knot. If, while fishing, you become snagged and have to break off, you don't want to be trying to tie a needle-knot whilst standing in the middle of a stream. The 12-in (0.3-m) length of 3 × nylon, with a tiny loop at the end, allows you to break off at the extreme tippet. It also enables you to change or lengthen your tippet quickly and easily.

Looking back on what has been said, it is very clear that the emphasis has been on lightness and delicacy. One accepts that this is always desirable in fishing, but on a small stream, working at close quarters and in shallow water, it is not only desirable but also absolutely necessary. Anything one can do to achieve this should be done. You will see in Fig. 3 that a plastic cast-connector is shown. This is just another aid – far better than a heavy knot or loop, or even a needle-knot.

Last but not least, we can consider the accessories that could be of use to us when fishing the stream. First among these must be the fishing vest, a wonderful invention and a real boon to a stream angler. It may not be so important to anglers fishing from a boat or the bank of a reservoir (they can rummage in a bag quite easily) but the convenience of having all you want immediately to hand in its own particular pocket is ideal when you are on the move.

A bag, or creel, is still useful for those larger items such as a thermos, sandwiches, or a spare spool for the reel, but if at

12

all possible use a wicker creel. It will do the same job as a bag, but nothing finer has ever come on the market to hold fish. The difference between fish kept in a closed bag and those on fresh fern in a creel is most striking.

Not all anglers these days carry a landing net. I used to feel undressed without mine but now it is invariably left in the car. This is because I so seldom keep any fish caught and prefer to unhook them in the water. I now realise how precious native trout have become. However, it is good practice to use a net when you wish to retain fish, and much safer when using very fine terminal tackle. Choose one that will fold and hang from your creel or belt. The habit of slinging it around your neck on an elastic cord so that it hangs down your back is dangerous on a small stream. It will catch in bankside vegetation then suddenly release giving you a terrific thump on the back.

The best type of net is one that opens out to a triangular shape, with two side-arms and a cord across the front edge. Make sure that brass has been used as much as possible in its construction – aluminium and plastic are poor substitutes. The net itself should be made of a synthetic rotproof material – and please, for the sake of the fish, no knots.

Before leaving the subject of tackle it might be as well to have a word about waders. Thigh waders are usually all that are required on a small stream. It is useful now and again to be able to wade just a little deeper, but chest-height waders are very cumbersome in wear and rather heavy going just to achieve those few extra inches. However, it's a personal choice and an angler may well wish to purchase waders that will be of use on other waters. I am, however, much more concerned with the soles of the waders than the length.

Rubber-cleated soles have no place on the rocky bed of a small stream, their only real use is for walking on dry land or on mud. The ideal sole for wading among slippery rocks and stones is thick, hard felt. This is very difficult to obtain in the UK, where you may have to make out the best you can with studded waders. The best type are those with studs that screw into a composition sole and can be easily replaced. When you buy waders try to buy spare studs at the same time.

For a long time I couldn't understand why I always seemed to slop water into my waders although I never wade deeper than several inches below the top edge. The problem lies in those very small studs and eyes that are situated on the inside and outside leg about 4 in (100 mm) from the top of the wader. If you look closely you will find that the centre of the stud is hollow and will allow water to pass through. Small rubber patches – from a bicycle repair-kit – placed on the inside of the wader will clear up this problem completely.

We haven't mentioned artificial flies, and for several good reasons. We will talk about these as we fish the stream. We can then find at first hand exactly what we require to obtain results. So, I think that's enough about tackle. Let's consider the quarry.

CHAPTER 3

THE QUARRY

It is intended here to discuss the various species of trout the angler may encounter whilst fishing small streams. A knowledge of our quarry, even a superficial one, is essential if we are to vary the tactics used to suit the species expected.

The common brown trout (*Salmo fario*), often referred to as the wild brownie, will most often be our quarry. This fish is a very ancient creature. Fossilised remains have been found that show it in the same form as today. Without doubt it has remained basically unchanged for many thousands of years. Many anglers consider the brown trout to be truly indigenous to the UK, and in a sense they are right, but the true position is that the brown trout is only a subspecies.

There is only one trout that is truly indigenous of the UK, and that is the sea trout (*S. trutta*). *S. fario* is a non-migratory subspecies. Many years ago it was the fashion to classify as a separate species all those trout from different regions and locations that differed in coloration and shape. The list was endless. An eminent scientist, Dr Tate Regan, working out of the British Museum, fully investigated this muddle and brought some order to it. Tate Regan found that the sea trout was the only indigenous trout to the UK, and that all others were of the same species regardless of differences in coloration, shape or specific location. True, even today, these subspecies are often given a scientific classification, but anglers must not be confused into thinking that they are fishing for anything other than varieties of *S. trutta*. The colour of a brown trout can vary enormously. Colour is due to a pigment in the skin – in fact it would be almost impossible to find two trout that were identical, even from the same water. The colour is influenced by the quality of the food available, the nature of the stream bed, the acidity or alkalinity of the water and the general health of the fish. Rich feeding results in brilliant large spots. Where an abundance of very rich food is available the spots are so large they tend to join together. Food that is rich in fats produces a substance called guanine that makes the fish decidedly silver in appearance. Alkaline water (pH 7.6–8.4) is usually rich in underwater vegetation and insect life. The result is trout that have a distinct silvery hue with large, brilliant spots present. Acid water (pH 4–6.8) is usually poor in food supply and produces trout much darker in appearance with many small, well-defined spots. In peaty or muddy water the trout can be very dark indeed.

There is a considerable difference between a naturally-dark fish from a water that normally produces dark fish, and the black appearance of a sick trout. Trout can suffer many internal ailments, some brought about by parasites and, of course, there is just plain old age. In all such cases the trout becomes either very pale, almost whitish in appearance, or so dark that it is almost black. Such trout are much better removed from the water and should never be returned to contaminate healthy fish.

Brown trout begin to deteriorate at about seven years of age and from that point on can be regarded as old fish. Several instances have been recorded of fish reaching over twelve years of age, but such instances are rare. The size the fish obtains in relation to its age depends entirely on its environment. As a general guide, a well-fed trout of 12 in

(0.3 m) will weigh $\frac{3}{4}$ lb (0.34 kg), a 15-in (0.4-m) trout $1\frac{1}{2}$ lb (0.7 kg) and one of 18 in (0.46 m) will weigh $2\frac{1}{2}$ lb (1.1 kg).

The trout's food consists in the main of living organisms that either live underwater or are taken off the surface. By far the bulk of a trout's diet is taken underwater. This must not be understood to mean that fishing with subsurface flies is the most productive method of taking trout – there are many times when only a dry fly will suffice. We should always be ready to vary our tactics according to the situation that confronts us. The chief items of food taken are flies that are hatched from the water or fall to its surface, underwater larvae, small crustaceans, worms and leeches, small fish-fry and green algae. Most of these items require clean, gravelly stream beds to thrive and flourish.

Colour plays a great part in a trout's life. It must be remembered that the trout lives in a drab environment, and practically all its food is drably coloured. Although a trout's colour vision cannot be doubted, it is not used to seeing bright, primary colours on a day-to-day basis. The primary colours of red, blue and yellow have no relation to the colours normally associated with food. The secondary colours of green, olive and purple are more in keeping with the trout's world, but by far the most natural to the fish are the tertiary colours of brown, olive and grey. When designing flies, tying flies or buying flies, these very important points about colour should be borne in mind.

Of course, flies tied in primary colours do have a place in our fly box, especially for use as attracters. In some cases flies of these colours are used deliberately to induce trout to attack such an unnatural intrusion into their world.

We must now consider the senses of the trout, especially as they affect us when fishing for them. These senses cannot be related to our own, for the fish has a totally-different bodily structure designed for living in an underwater world. However, many of the senses possessed by the fish we can readily recognise; others are subject to conjecture. The trout's lateral line and skin surface are made up of a complex nervous system that enables it to pick up vibrations over a considerable distance. The lateral line also enables the fish to ascertain the direction of the current and the pressure of the water. This latter facility assists the trout to avoid unseen obstacles when it is fighting to avoid capture.

Although vibrations are not the same as hearing as we know it, the result is practically the same. Aided by the earstones situated at the rear of its brain, the trout is able to 'hear' all noises that cause even the slightest vibration. Footfalls on the bank, splashing water, dropped tackle, the impact of a line on water – they are all 'heard' by the trout. External noises that cause no underwater vibration, such as talking, shouting, motor horns, etc., are not picked up by the trout.

The sense of taste is absent in the trout as they possess no taste buds. Their food is taken quickly by sight – taste does not enter into it at all. It would be completely useless to try to give an artificial fly any sort of flavour. However, trout do possess olfactory organs that pick up odours. They are attracted by some odours and repelled by others. This sense is entirely different from an air-breathing animal and has no connection with the breathing process that, in the case of the trout, is performed through the gills. To illustrate how this last sense can affect the angler I offer myself as an example. I love my pipe and invariably puff away contentedly whilst fishing – it is an admirable insect repellant – but I am always very careful to rinse off my fingers after filling my pipe and before touching any of my flies. It is a wise safety precaution.

It is often said that the trout's sense of vision is acute. Before we take this statement for granted let's consider several facts: the fish has no means to adjust the pupils of the eyes as a protection against bright light, nor has it eyelids or eyelashes to shade the eyes. Consequently, bright light has a dazzling effect. It has no binocular vision to aid in judging distances, and the panoramic vision it does possess makes it impossible to focus both eyes at the same time on a particular object. The eyes are also tilted forward and upwards so that it is practically impossible to see objects below and behind. Nevertheless, be in no doubt that the eyesight of a trout is perfectly designed for its needs: it is up to us to take advantage of the deficiencies.

When fishing, try to keep the sun behind you, making sure, of course, not to cast a shadow over the fish. At the same time remember that a fly cast to a shaded area is seen much more acutely than one in bright sunlight, which slightly dazzles the trout. As our business is to deceive, the less chance we give it for close examination the better.

Due to the trout's cone of vision, an angler some 30 ft (9.1 m) from the fish is invisible provided no part of the angler is more than 5 ft (1.5 m) above water level. When wading, our upper torso is considerably less than 5 ft (1.5 m) and we can approach the trout in the assurance that we cannot be seen within a 10-yard (9.2-m) cast. However, be warned that the vibrations we make are a different matter and can be picked up by the fish long before we are within casting distance. We also have the advantage of being unseen when we are below and behind the fish as all trout naturally lie facing upstream.

From time to time we may well encounter other trout than wild brownies. Many small streams have sea-trout runs, and although the pursuit of sea trout is a specialist activity beyond the scope of this book, we may well encounter these fish whilst angling for our brownies. Most serious sea-trout fishing takes place at night. They are extremely shy when in fresh water and usually lie resting in the deeper pools, but this does not mean that they will not take food during daylight hours. If we are stealthy in our approach, and are fishing the wet fly, there are the rare occasions when these fish are accidentally taken. They are magnificent fighters, and although it may well be beyond the capabilities of our very light tackle to hold a good-size sea trout, we may be able to land one of the smaller ones. There is no way these fish, fresh from the sea, can be confused with a brown trout. They are bright silver in appearance and the spots are small and inclined to be black.

The sea-trout smolt, that is to say the young sea trout that has never been to sea, is a different matter. After birth they remain in fresh water for between three and five years, and usually reach the size of approximately 8 in (200 mm) before migrating to sea. At this stage they are almost impossible to distinguish from small, wild brownies and are often mistaken as such.

The rainbow trout – a native of North America – will be found in many streams and rivers of the UK. In the main these are hatchery fish placed as stock to be fished for on a put-and-take basis. The writer knows of only three rivers in the UK where the rainbow trout has become acclimatised and now thrives and spawns in the normal way. Apart from the aforementioned three rivers, all rainbow stock-fish are hatchery bred by artificial means.

These fish are truly beautiful in appearance, predominantly silver with a myriad of black spots extending into the tail. They have a band of iridescent rainbow colours the length of the body – hence the name. On the North American continent there are two species of these fish: *S. shasta* is the non-migratory species, *S. gairdneri* being the seagoing steelhead. In their natural habitat these fish grow to a considerable size, weights in double figures being quite common. They were introduced into the UK in 1882, no great care being taken as to which species were imported. The hatcheries also treated both the species as being identical; consequently, cross-breeding resulted during the artificial egg-stripping and fertilisation processes. The result is the cross-bred rainbow prevalent in the UK today, classified as *S. irideus*.

The rainbow trout is an aggressively greedy fish that consumes approximately twice the food of the brown trout, and puts on weight accordingly. A well-fed rainbow will increase in weight by well over 1 lb (0.5 kg) per year. In fact, hatchery-reared fish have well exceeded that figure. However, its life-span is short and very few rainbows live beyond six years of age.

There is no doubt that the rainbow is an ideal stock fish for put-and-take still-water fisheries, but the writer questions the wisdom of river managements using the fish for the same purpose in preference to brown trout. Even the cross-bred rainbow still has a decided wanderlust and constantly tries to drop downstream. They will not reproduce themselves, and they certainly give the indigenous brownies a hard time in the contest for food. At the risk of bringing the wrath of many down on our heads, may we suggest that the motive behind such stocking is purely to obtain instant large fish without too much regard for the damage done to the natural fishery? Otherwise, why not stock browns?

When fishing for rainbows the angler should keep in mind the few basic instincts that are peculiar to this fish. Rainbows are considerably more aggressive than browns and will often freely attack brightly coloured flies that the brown will not look at. They are also constantly on the lookout for food and are not nearly as selective as browns. However, when a hatch is in progress they are as selective as any other trout. When a rainbow is hooked they often become spectacular fighters – be prepared for a number of jumps out of the water – and they are very deceiving when they come to the net. Be prepared for an apparently spent fish to become suddenly alive again, even jumping over the net!

The last fish to be discussed is one that you may never come into contact with. The brook trout (*S. salvelinus*

The brook trout (*S. salvelinus fontinalis*). This
beautiful fish, taken from a Canadian water, has scarlet
fins edged with white, green marbled back, and brilliant
red sides and belly. Brook trout have now been introduced
into the UK – but although first results are promising it is
really too early to judge results

fontinalis) is not really a trout at all, scientifically speaking he
is a char. This truly magnificent fish – its spawning colours
are unbelievable – is a native of the Eastern Seaboard of the
USA and Canada. He is the flyfishers' ideal: a fantastically
beautiful appearance, a very strong fighter, a very free riser,
and a succulent meal on the table.

During the last few years the brook trout has been
introduced into the UK and has made its appearance at
several put-and-take still-water fisheries. As yet it has not
been introduced into running water. It has been said that
UK streams are not cold enough to support this fish, and
that may be true as far as its spawning habits are concerned.

However, the writer can vouch for the fact that many North American streams populated with this fish become far warmer during summer than the average stream in the UK. Without doubt experiments will be made in the future and, who knows, perhaps in time we will all have the opportunity to fish for this near-perfect quarry.

It is now time to put our tackle to use to see if we are able to catch a few of these trout.

CHAPTER 4

FISHING TACTICS

(1)

As we approach the stream it would be a good idea for you to have a look at the diagram in Fig. 4. This is not an imaginary stream, it's one of my favourites, one where I fish whenever I have the opportunity. It has its source high in the hills of South Wales, then it meanders its way down a most beautiful, wooded valley before it flows into one of the major rivers of the area. Sea trout make their way up the stream during the appropriate season and during the day lie in the deeper pools. These upper reaches, where we will fish today, abound with wild brownies. No stocking takes place here – all the fish are stream bred – and are the most beautifully-marked fish I have ever seen.

In the early season, and after heavy rain, this stream becomes a minor torrent, but at other times it is low and clear and most attractive. We have picked the best time of day for mid-season, early afternoon. Sometimes at this time of year, depending on the weather, very early morning is also good, but it must be very early, at first light with the mist still on the water. When the sun comes up fish seem to go off the feed until after midday. I hope we will have the opportunity to fish here again during the early season and again at the tail end. We will then find the mornings and late evenings will suit us best.

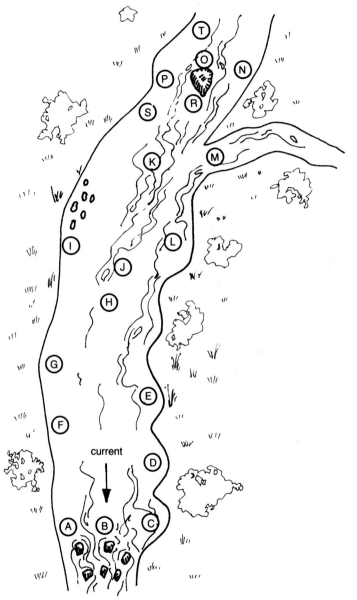

Fig. 4 Locations for tactics (1)

Excellent dry fly fishing can often be found on a lowland
pasture water where the long glassy glides hide
many good brownies

Well, here we are. We will approach the water at point A.
This may not be the best stretch available to us, but it will
give us a chance to get the feel of our tackle. From point A
to H the stream is of uniform depth, about 3 ft (0.9 m) to 4 ft
(1.2 m), with quite a good current; the stream bed is clearly
visible and made up of stone and gravel; and there is no
underwater plant-life to speak of. The banks are quite over-
grown, but that won't worry us unduly if we are careful.

It's what might be described as a small pool, and good
dry-fly water. You look discouraged, is it because it's clear
and shallow and you can't see any fish? Don't let it put you
off. At midday with sun on the water, no self-respecting
brownie is going to lie out there clearly in view, they are
much too wary for that. They are around all right, but we
have to locate them.

'x' denotes Trout

Fig. 5 The complete overhang

This is another favourite trout lie – but an extremely difficult one to fish from either bank. Very often a dry fly floated down to the fish from an upstream position is the only tactic possible

Let's study the situation carefully. There are a lot of small insects about, midges mostly, but no obvious hatch of aquatic flies. I can't see any rise-forms either, so not much interest is being shown in the midges.

Wait a minute – that was quite a nice rise under that far bank at point C – did you see it? It must have been to some land-blown insect, or perhaps a beetle or caterpillar fell from those overhanging branches. Well, that's encouraging, at least we know where one brownie is.

During these hot, bright afternoons the fish usually lie fairly dormant unless a hatch develops. A favourite spot is in the shade and close to the bank, especially if there are overhanging branches. They are seldom completely

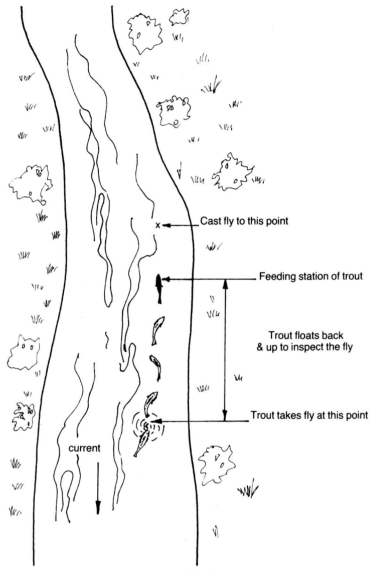

Cast fly to this point

Feeding station of trout

Trout floats back
& up to inspect the fly

Trout takes fly at this point

current

Fig. 6 The rise

Note The rise-form you see is downstream of the trout's feeding station. After taking the fly, the trout invariably returns to his original feeding station

28

dormant and any juicy morsel that comes their way is very often immediately snapped up.

A rise to a fly being brought down by the current is usually a short distance downstream from the trout's feeding position. This is because a trout floats 'backwards and upwards' as he takes a fly, and also because by the time you see the rise-form it has passed downstream from where it actually occurred. A rise to a land-blown insect can be quite different. The insect suddenly lands on the water and the reaction of the trout is often just as sudden – a quick swirl and the insect has gone.

I think that if we make a careful cast to where that rise occurred we might strike lucky. Try a spider fly, they usually work quite well when there is no hatch in progress and one is prospecting for trout, as we are. You have never heard of a spider fly? Well, I have a few in my box, try this black-and-white one. They can be tied in a number of combinations to suit the conditions one finds at different times during the season – we'll have a talk about them after we've finished fishing.

That was a nice cast, just right. Don't forget to control your slack line immediately – *too late*! He took it against all that slack line and your reaction was far too slow, now all you have is a drowned fly. Never mind, let the fly continue downstream for a while before you recover it, there will be much less disturbance that way.

You will have to watch that slack-line recovery, these small stream brownies take very fast and it's important to be in a position to strike quickly. A hard strike isn't at all necessary, just a tightening of the line, but that's very hard to do if there is a lot of slack line out. I find that the best way is to hold the line between thumb and forefinger of the right hand as you grip the rod. Then, with your left hand, draw in line and let it drop at your feet. That way you have a reasonable contact with the fly as it comes downstream towards you. A fish always turns down after taking a fly and just tightening the line is usually sufficient to hook him.

We will let that fish rest for a bit. I don't think he was too disturbed, probably he didn't feel the hook at all, he just didn't like the taste of the fly. We can cast to him again after a short while.

If we wade a few paces out into the stream – very gently so that we make no disturbance – we will be in a nice position to cast a short line under our own bank to point F, but first make a couple of false casts to dry off that drowned fly. There is no need for more than that, a spider fly rarely needs any floatant – that's one of the advantages of using them.

Nicely done, that was another good cast. Look how high that spider fly rides on the water, they are so easy to see with that white front hackle. That's a lot better, keep control of the slack as the fly – *got him*!

Nice and easy, keep control of the line, don't hold him too hard though, just draw in the line with your left hand – forget about the reel – now you have him. Beautiful isn't he? Look at that golden hue, and those lovely red spots, a genuine wild brownie! Just over $\frac{1}{2}$ lb (0.2 kg), but I am sure we can do better than that. Let's slip him back so that he can grow a little more.

Have you noticed what a mess he has made of the fly? Always make it a rule to clean up a fly thoroughly before you recommence fishing. I know it's a temptation when you are excited to cast again immediately, but it doesn't pay. You must take a few moments to reorganise and assess the situation. That fly needs work on it before it will do its job again. Rinse it off in the water below us, then squeeze it dry in a piece of cloth before you re-arrange the hackles. That's a lot better. After I squeeze them dry I often dip them in silicone powder. It's not essential but it does a lovely job of perking up the hackle. Make a couple of false-casts and we are back in business.

Do you feel like having another go at that fish over at point C? If he's still there he might be willing to oblige us again. You can cast quite easily from here. That's the idea – right on target. Keep in contact. No, nothing – he didn't even look at it. Never mind, let the fly continue downstream before you recover it. A false-cast then try again, nothing is disturbed so far. Good, another nice cast, draw in the slack as the fly – *tighten! – you have him!*

Watch out – he's going straight for the fast water behind us. Lay the rod over level with the water and apply sidestrain. That's better, now he's back in the pool. You're holding him too tightly! Look at all that commotion he's making on the surface! Good, good, he's coming in. Keep a fairly tight line, hand-line him and let the line drop at your feet. That's right, nicely done. He's all yours. That's a fine fish, he certainly gave us a little excitement. Isn't he lovely? I can never get over how beautiful they are. You want to keep him? I agree, he'll make a nice supper, pop him into your bag.

Now you can see what I meant when I said that line-backing is rarely needed – even a good-size fish can only use the natural obstacles and snags in a small stream – it's a matter of control rather than having lots of backing. You don't have much chance to play them from the reel either, hand-lining gives you a much better control.

Well, I must say we have really disturbed the fishing in this pool with all that commotion on the surface. I would imagine that any other fish in the pool have headed upstream and have probably disturbed the fish up there as well. We'll climb out of the water and sit on the bank for a smoke. Afterwards we can walk further upstream to point I.

Here we are at point I. Although the bank is steep we can climb down to the stream quite easily and stand among the rocks. The water is only a few inches deep near the bank.

This stretch of water is very interesting: see that small inlet

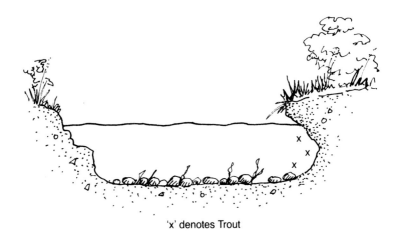

'x' denotes Trout

Fig. 7 The undercut bank
A fly has to be cast as close to the bank as possible to tempt any trout in these positions

over at point M? It is a disused millrace. Years ago a mill used to stand over there and that inlet was probably the equal of another small stream. Now it's more like a drainage ditch. Just the same, there is still a fair flow of water through it and it has, over the years, dug out quite a deep channel between points K and J. With the combined flow of the stream and the inlet, the current is quite fast. It has also left an eddy of fairly slack water at point L. This is due to the fact that in spate conditions that inlet becomes a gushing torrent and the bank over at point L has been well undercut. I would think there is a fairly deep hole there.

The depth, of course, depends on the time of year. With the water low as it is now I doubt that the channel is more than 4 ft (1.2 m) deep. There are a number of small rocks on the bed of the channel – you can tell this from the rough surface of the water. Consequently, although good-size fish don't like fighting current to obtain food, here in the channel

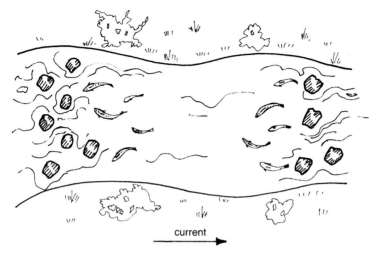

Fig. 8 The head and tail of a pool

Trout lie at both the head and tail of a pool. The largest fish always lead the group and have first choice of the food washed down

the turbulence on the surface caused by the rock appears a little downstream of the rock's true position

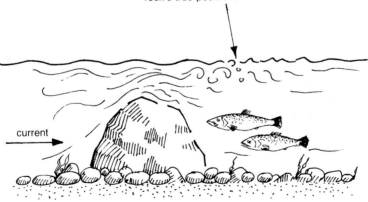

Fig. 9 The underwater rock

A favourite trout lie. There is no necessity to fight the current. Food particles pass clearly overhead and are easily taken

33

they have shelter behind the small rocks – and can still see what passes overhead. It looks like good water to me. Of course, the undercut bank over at point L must be a good holding station for a fish or two: near enough to the main current for a continuous food supply; little current to fight; and, most importantly of all – safe shelter.

As a matter of interest, you will rarely find small fish in a hole like that at point L. It is such a good feeding station that it is usually taken by one or two of the bigger trout who chase out all the small-fry. If you ever catch a trout from such a position his place is immediately taken by the next fish in line of a similar size. Consequently, it's always a good spot to return to.

We will fish the main channel first, and leave the eddy at point L undisturbed until last. We could try our spider fly, but I don't have the same faith in it when it's used on broken water. I always feel that its visibility is impaired. As there is still nothing obviously hatching, I would suggest a 'high-wing variant'. Yes, I know that is also probably new to you, but don't let it bother you now – we said we would have a long chat on flies later, after we finish fishing. Try this one. Looks a bit odd? Let's hope it doesn't look that odd to the fish.

We will work the channel in four quarters, lower left, lower right, then upper left, finishing with upper right. Yes, you have the idea, that way our casts don't disturb the water to be fished at a later stage. You will really have to have your wits about you, rises in fast water are very hard to see – let's see how we get on.

So, the lower left of the channel first. That cast was all right, but the line is out of control. It must be drawn in as the fly comes downstream towards you, otherwise the fly will very quickly start dragging in this fast current. Notice how the 'high wing' of our fly stands out? That's not the reason for it – but it's a nice added bonus, at least you will see if it's taken. Not much luck so far, try the far side of the channel.

That was a rise! Didn't you see it? It obviously took you unawares. No good striking afterwards, I told you they would be fast. The current makes them even faster. Try again.

Another rise! Yes, you were quick enough that time. Bad luck you missed him, I don't think it was your fault. In fast water it often happens that way, sometimes it's a very small fish that fails to take the fly properly – eyes probably larger than its stomach, but larger fish also mistime in fast water. Keep trying, at least we are getting some action.

Not much good trying to hook that one. Did you see how high he jumped out of the water to take the fly? All 5 ins (125 mm) of him! Just as well he missed!

We don't seem to be getting what we're after in this fast water. It's often the way that when the youngsters are in action the larger fish stay down and out of the competition. I have noticed that the reverse is also true: when larger fish are surface feeding, the small ones seem to have been chased away. I think that we would be best advised to leave well alone, otherwise we will be plagued with these little fish – and I hate to see them hooked, it nearly always results in damage to them. Let's pay some attention to that eddy over at point L.

You want to change back to a spider fly? Why not? We will be fishing fairly slack water, and it has brought the best results so far.

Have you considered the problem of the fast current between us and point L? It's going to cause the fly to drag almost immediately when, in fact, what we are after is for the fly to linger in the eddy. There is no way of avoiding it either, our line will have to pass over that fast current. You might try a 'hook-cast' – not too difficult, it only sounds difficult. On the final forward-cast, just as the line extends – but before the fly touches the water – shoot a little line, and at the same time twist the rod round to the left. It's the twist bit that's hard to understand. The best way to imagine it is to think of turning the hand that grips the rod so that the reel is pointing out to the right. Got the idea? Try it, if done properly the fly should land where you intended – but the line will have an upstream belly in it – we hope the fly will do its job before the line straightens out. Dont's forget that you will need to strike a little harder to compensate for the slack line that's out.

Not bad at all, a nice curve to the line. Don't watch the line, watch the fly! *Strike! Strike hard!*

You have him! Don't try to bring him in through the fast water, let him go downstream a little. Yes, I know it's bad practice to play a fish downstream, but it's better than pulling him through fast water. Gently does it, work him over to our side. Gently – you are playing the current as well

'x' denotes normal lies

Fig. 10 Evening feeding in the shallows

During a summer evening trout will feed on the shallow flats. A very stealthy approach is necessary to get within casting distance – or they are gone, like shadows, back to their normal lies

as the fish. That's better, now we can wade down towards him. Lively, isn't he? He wants to go again. Give him a little line and let him go, he can't have much fight left. Nice fish! Better than the one in the bag. Keep him, it will make a nice brace.

If we move upstream a bit, past these rocks and towards point S, we will be able to cast to the mouth of the inlet at point M. I have never found any large fish there, it seems to be a favourite spot for the youngsters to sport themselves in the very fast water. Try a high-wing fly – one about size-18 hook should serve well – then if they are very small they won't be damaged.

Well, I did warn you of the possible results, two miniature trout is not much to show for all your efforts, but it does show how your reactions have speeded up – those fast splashy rises are very hard to strike.

Yes, I know that large protruding rock upstream looks tempting, but I wouldn't bother with it now if I were you. Think about it. Any trout sheltering behind that rock – and

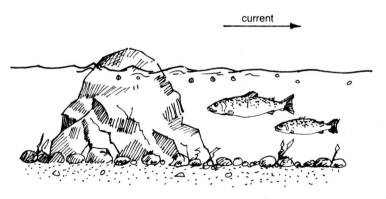

current

Fig. 11 The protruding rock

Provides good shelter for trout from fast currents. No food can pass directly overhead – therefore a dry fly is of little use. A wet fly, worked deep round the base of the rock, could bring good results

37

I am sure there must at least be one or two – cannot be in a position to surface feed. They can't see anything coming downstream because of the rock and nothing passes directly overhead. It's all swept to the side and past them before they could even start a rise. It's a poor position for feeding on anything except food that is deep down among the stones. Trout pick that sort of spot to lay up and rest. One day we will have a go at it from upstream with a wet fly – that might be a different story.

How about calling it a day? We can have a drink at that little pub on the way home and talk about flies.

CHAPTER 5

SPIDERS AND VARIANTS

To understand fully the theory behind the flies we use, it is necessary to consider the eternal controversy over the merits of exact imitation versus flies designed to attract. Obviously, the ideal artificial fly to use is the one that perfectly imitates the natural insect. No one would dispute the desirability of this when the trout are selectively feeding on one particular insect to the exclusion of all others. However, who knows what constitutes a perfect imitation? Certainly no artificial fly ever tied by man even approaches an exact imitation, nor will it ever do so. It does not look an exact imitation to our human eye, let alone to a trout who is an expert on these things.

The champions of exact imitation, carefully selecting their materials, meticulously blending their colours, are not even in a position to tell us if the trout is able to see colours in the same way that they do. In fact, there is solid evidence to the contrary. Further, no fly-tying material has ever been found that will imitate the body of a natural insect in a truly satisfactory manner. As for shape, the artificial does not have the slightest resemblance to the natural – and that statement is true even when one disregards the hook on which it is tied.

The argument is then put forward that the artificial truly gives the 'impression' of the natural, as it meets those requirements of colour, shape and size. Does it? The answer must be that we just don't know – size perhaps, but shape and colour are very debatable. In the matter of shape we have already acknowledged that the artificial does not resemble the natural – and colour is definitely an unknown quantity.

What colours does a trout see? A trout's eyes are for underwater viewing. What exactly does he see when looking through his world of water, past the surface, into our world? Can he see images above the water-line clearly? We don't know the answers to these questions.

At this stage we might well ask, why does the trout take our artificials at all? A good question, but take them he does, and many times without any hesitation whatsoever. In some way the artificial must clearly imitate the natural – but in what way?

With intensive research, we could probably come up with a minimum of 700 artificial-fly patterns. Each of these patterns have probably taken dozens of fish, if not more. Why so many patterns? We certainly don't have that many natural flies. What is the common denominator to all these artificials, all so differently coloured, none of them exact imitations? A very difficult question to answer – we have already dismissed shape and colour, we are left only with size. Surely it can't be size!

We are, however, left with another factor to consider – the general 'form' of the artificial. That perhaps creates an illusion of a natural insect.

This thought may lead us somewhere, let's pursue it. If the trout does not see an artificial above the water-line clearly, if he only sees a hazy illusion with the colour and size only just discernible, can that be enough? It might well be that he does not perhaps see the natural much better. Who can tell? It would certainly account for some of the weird things trout at times take off the surface – I once heard of a cigarette end!

So, we have come full circle: 'the ideal artificial fly to use is the one that perfectly imitates the natural insect'. If we bear in mind that the natural itself may be only a hazy object, then an illusion of that hazy object is, in fact, a perfect imitation. Could we have found the solution? I'm afraid we will never really know – and it's just as well – or there wouldn't be any trout left to fish for.

We can now consider the spider fly in the light of the above comments, for the spider fly is designed purely and simply to create such an illusion. I take no credit for the design of the spider fly, it originated in the USA many years ago. It is the natural successor of a fly designed in the late nineteenth century, called a Neversink skater, named after the Neversink River in Upper New York State, a stream in the Catskill Mountains. The Neversink skater is essentially a spider fly without a tail. Thus the hackles spread over the surface of the water while the hook hangs downwards. The fly was

Spider

41

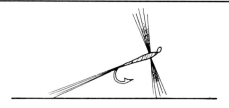

Fig. 12 The spider fly

designed for very low, clear-water conditions in bright sunlight. I have, personally, used the fly in such conditions in the Catskill Mountains, and can vouch for its effectiveness – fishing the fly in a few inches of water in bright sunlight, I have seen large trout swim out from under the bank to take the fly.

The addition of a tail to the Neversink skater (and thus the birth of the spider fly), was to enable the fly to be used in places where there was an appreciable current. However, the conditions for which it was designed remained the same – low, bright, very clear water. Lifting the hook above the water also enabled a small body of gold tinsel to be added. This was to enhance and complete the illusion: the light on the tinsel above the water-line giving a hazy transluscence when viewed through water from below (see Fig. 12).

At the end of this chapter I have given various dressings for the spider fly. These are my own, based on my own experiences with the spider. However, bear in mind that there are no standard dressings for the fly, it's a design only – use your own combinations, it's a lot of fun.

The 'high-wing variant' is a different matter. Here I must plead guilty and accept full responsibility. A trout taking surface food in shallow water has, by virtue of being close to the surface, a very small 'viewing window'. In fast water this gives the trout very little time to make a decision to rise, especially as he gets almost no advance warning of an approaching insect through surface indentations. Due to the

The 'high-wing variant'

refraction of light, he is able to see an object that is higher than the water-line just before it enters his 'viewing window' – how soon before depends upon the height of the object.

So, the 'high-wing variant' was born, and the result was most gratifying (see Fig. 13). I use this tying on all standard

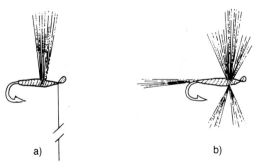

a)   b)

Fig. 13 The 'high-wing variant'

(a) Shows the high wing tied in position as the first stage of tying the fly
(b) Shows the completed fly – finished off as any standard fly pattern

43

flies, of course omitting the usual split wings where called for in the pattern. The best materials for the 'high wing' are mallard or teal-feather fibres, tied in as a bunch so that the height is one-and-a-half times the length of the hook shank. The fibres are not separated into separate wings. This is entirely unnecessary: most natural insects carry their wings closed. After tying in the 'high wing' the fly is finished off in the usual way and it will be found that winding the hackle in front of the 'high wing' helps keep it upright and slightly spread.

A point about the wing fibres. For some reason (I am not at all sure why) the trout seem to prefer mallard-feather fibre that is bronze in colour. The difference this colour makes is quite outstanding. However, natural mallard fibre in this colour is very hard to find, and some years back I soaked a number of these feathers in a solution of cold coffee – the result was exactly what is required and I am still using the same feathers today.

Now we must consider the question of which standard patterns are best given the high-wing treatment. As mentioned before, the number of fly patterns are legion and all will take trout under certain conditions. The trouble is that at other times they are almost ineffective: the fly has yet to be invented that will kill at all times under all conditions – and it is a good thing for our sport that this is so.

However, we still have to make the decision as to what flies to have in our fly box. One way over this dilemma – and a very good way – is to use those flies that are considered good local flies in the area where one is fishing. I have no idea why a trout, say, from Yorkshire, should have a preference for one fly while his cousin, say, from Wales, prefers another. Certainly the insect-life does not vary to that extent from region to region, and even if it did we have already considered that these flies are a long way from being an exact imitation. Still, it is a definite fact that certain flies produce very good consistent results in certain areas. Sometimes it is not even the pattern that is different, it is just the way the fly is tied that seems to achieve results.

Most local angling-club secretaries, or local tackle-shops, will advise on a fly selection that is considered right for the area. These patterns can then be tied by the angler in the high-wing mode, or ordered that way from his usual supplier.

What has been said may, to a certain extent, serve to cut down the necessity of carrying literally dozens of fly patterns, but it does not solve the most important question of all – size. Remember what we said about the fly being a 'hazy impression'? If the fly is the wrong size the impression it gives must be very much impaired, no matter how else it resembles the natural insect. In consequence, it is essential to have each pattern in a variety of sizes. In practice, I have found three sizes will serve quite well, and my choice is usually for hook sizes 14, 16 and 18.

It is unfortunate that many amateur fly-tyers, as well as many professionals, seem to be oblivious to the fact that if a fly is tied on a certain hook then the general size of the fly must be in proportion. One sees the same-size hackle, the same-size tail, etc., on flies of all hook sizes. This makes the variation of hook size a complete farce. I strongly advise against this practice, and would certainly refuse to accept such flies from a professional supplier.

Before leaving the subject of flies I would like to make a plea to all tackle manufacturers: when are we going to see a fly box that is made with compartments, or has the depth, that will take our flies without crushing them beyond recognition?

Enough said. Let's think about our next fishing trip.

Dressings for the spider fly

Black and white spider (LS)

Hook: 14, 16 or 18 standard dry fly.
Body: Two or three turns of gold tinsel.
Tail: Stiff, black-hackle fibres – long.
Hackle: Two turns of black hackle, fronted by two turns of white hackle.

Brown and white spider (LS)

Hook: 14, 16 or 18 standard dry fly.
Body: Two or three turns of gold tinsel.
Tail: Stiff, ginger-hackle fibres – long.
Hackle: Two turns of barred, plymouth-rock hackle (or ginger), fronted by two turns of white hackle.

Grey and white spider (LS)

Hook: 14, 16 or 18 standard dry fly.
Body: Two or three turns of gold tinsel.
Tail: Stiff, blue-dun- (or grizzle-) hackle fibres – long.
Hackle: Two turns of blue-dun (or grizzle) hackle, fronted by two turns of white hackle.

Pale evening spider (LS)

Hook: 14, 16 or 18 standard dry fly.
Body: Olive tying-silk only.
Tail: Stiff, cream-hackle fibres – long.
Hackle: Three or four turns of cream badger (with good black centre to the hackle).

CHAPTER 6

FISHING TACTICS
(2)

I'm glad you were available to come fishing today. I particularly wanted to take advantage of the recent rain – two days of heavy rainfall should have made quite a difference to the state of the water. I thought we might go back to the little Welsh stream where we fished before. This time we can use wet flies.

Many fine brownies have been taken from
this typical wet fly water

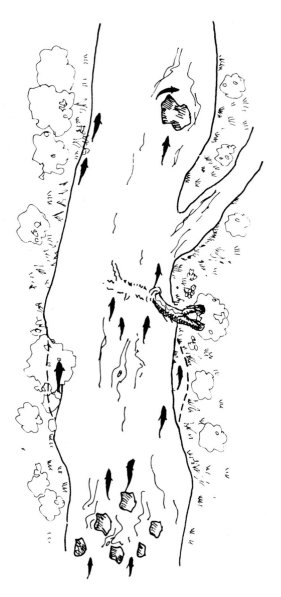

Fig. 14 Favourite trout lies

We picked a good day for it, nice to see the sun out again with everything looking so green and fresh. It's very muddy underfoot along the bank so I expect the water to be a little coloured.

Yes, look at how coloured the water is. You can't see the bottom anywhere, and it's much higher than I expected. These small streams react to rain much more than the larger rivers, but usually they clear down much more quickly afterwards. Let's walk along the bank to point T above that large protruding rock where we finished up last time.

Look at that rock now! Only an inch or so above the surface. The water must be up at least 6 in (150 mm). You can imagine what it must have been like immediately after the rain. The current is very strong too. We will have to be careful as we wade – you can't see where to put your feet and I hate wading like that.

It's not so easy to climb down the bank now it's all mud. Pass your rod down first in case you stumble or slip. It's a fact of life that if you stumble you nearly always fall on the rod!

Good, all safely down. There's not much room to cast here, we are too close to the bank and it's not possible to wade out into the main stream. It's a good job we are going to fish wet fly downstream, we will be able to roll-cast most of the time.

We will need to use a sinkant on our leader. I usually use a mixture of fuller's earth and washing-up liquid made up as a paste – not on all the leader, just the last 2 or 3 ft (0.6 or 0.9 m). Use a little on the fly as well, then rinse it partially off in the stream.

What fly to use? Well, even though the water is coloured I would still use a fairly drab fly: remember these are brownies and they are not too partial to gaudy flies even under these conditions. They are able to see in coloured water much better than you think and are expecting natural food to be brought down by the current. They don't need to be induced to take. Something like a lead-wing coachman would be a good fly to start with.

Strip a few yards of line off the reel and shake it out through the rod rings so that it floats downstream under our own bank – about 12 yd (11 m) is enough. While it straightens out we can look things over and plan our campaign.

That fast water in the channel between the rock and the bank, at point N, looks particularly good, but let's fish this side of the rock first. Always fish the closer spots first so that you keep the disturbance down to a minimum. We will cast to point O and let the current take the fly around this side of the rock to point R.

A good roll-cast will do the job nicely. You're not quite sure how it's done? It's not at all difficult, really. You already have the line out downstream nice and straight. Draw it towards you by raising the rod tip and at the same time extending your arm upwards – your rod and arm should now be almost vertical with some line hanging down in a curve. Let the rod angle drift slightly backwards, not too much – then bring the rod arm down smartly so as to snap the rod in the direction you wish the fly to go. The whole cast must be one continuous action, no jerky movements and no pauses. Try it for yourself.

See, the line rolled out in a loop directly to point O, no problem at all. Knowing how to make a good roll-cast is half the battle on these small streams. You will find many places where you can't make a normal back-cast and a roll-cast is the only way to get the line out.

We had no response to that cast. Let the line straighten out below us so that we are in a position to roll-cast again. This time we will give a little action to the fly as it swims round the rock. We can do this by jiggling the line a little with the left hand and at the same time giving little jerks to the rod tip. The fly will then dart about as it swims downstream.

We must keep an eye on the upper part of the leader that is floating on the surface: a take as the fly travels downstream will rarely be felt on the line. If you see any unusual movement of the upper leader – a slight dip or a pause – then strike. There is very little in a stream that will impede a wet fly swimming in the current. Any unusual movement is most likely to be a fish.

No response again? Never mind, let the line continue on its way downstream and swing across in the current. What, you felt a tug as it swung across? I'm not surprised. As the line straightens out the fly rises to the surface in an arc and this is very attractive to the small fry. Sometimes they hook themselves, but mostly they only pluck at it. Mind you, it's not always small-fry, but you will soon know if it is a larger fish as the take is then very definite. You will feel a good pull and the fish is nearly always hooked.

I think the tendency of the small-fry to snatch at a rising fly is probably the reason downstream fishing with a wet fly is not permitted on some rivers. I suppose one could use a much larger fly – say a size 10 or 8 – but I feel that a smaller hook, size 14 or 16, has much better holding power. A large hook is inclined to saw away and create a hole, or tear out. These smaller hooks dig in nicely. Of course, it's all relative to the size of fish expected.

Try a cast over to that channel at point N. You will have to flip your line over the rock as soon as the cast is completed otherwise it will not be able to travel downstream. It's easy to do, just swing the rod tip over with a flick – it's called mending the cast.

Nicely done, now you have made a roll-cast with a mend. Remember to keep the fly working – that's right – and keep a sharp eye on that piece of floating leader.

You have him! You saw that little pull as quickly as I did. Hand-line him in, just as we did before. He's a good one. You will have to let him go a little, he's playing deep and that's a sign of a good fish. Try to get him out of the main current into slack water behind the rock. Good, he's well under control. Pass me your net and gently draw him over it – he's all yours! That's a very good fish for this water, larger than the fish you kept the last time. Beautifully coloured, thick across the shoulder, he'll make a very good meal. Put him into the bag.

I suggest we move downstream a bit to point P, I don't think we'll get another fish out of that channel today.

Now we are at point P you will be able to roll-cast to just above the mouth of the inlet at point M, then let your cast swing round in the current to point K. Keep the cast fairly short so that you don't disturb that undercut bank below the inlet, we want to fish there later.

A good cast, that roll-cast is coming along very well. Don't forget to keep working the fly as it swims downstream. Nothing this time, let the line straighten out ready for the next roll-cast.

That inlet is a minor torrent and it's really churning up the main stream. I don't think the fly is working deep enough, the current is keeping it close to the surface. We really want to be about 4 ft (1.2 m) deep. Have you a weighted fly in your box?

I always prefer to use a weighted fly in preference to a split shot on the leader. When a split shot is used it practically destroys the darting action of the fly, and casting becomes quite difficult – especially with the roll-cast.

Not much weight is needed, far less than you think. When I tie my own flies I just put a few turns of copper wire round the hook shank before the body is completed. I used to use fine, lead wire, but even in the fine grades it is too heavy. If you order weighted flies make sure you specify 'lightly weighted' – the average commercial weighted fly is a monstrosity.

Here, I haven't a weighted lead-wing coachman but this

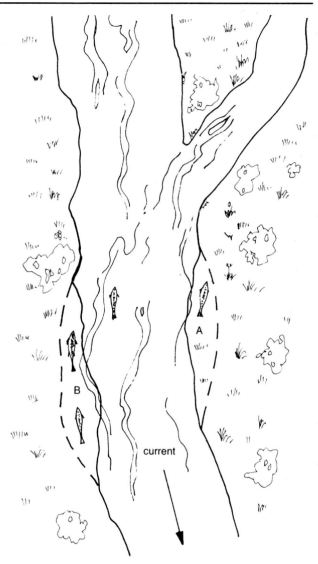

Fig. 15 Confluence with tributary
Trout find the influx of food satisfactory, but need to lie out of the direct current.
Eddies at A and B are favourite lies
Note Eddies at both A and B probably have undercut banks
caused by past spates

53

weighted hare's-ear might do the job. It's a good all-round fly, especially good in high water.

Ready? Let's make the same cast again. That's much better, see how the leader has all but disappeared? That fly is well down just where we want it to be. Keep it working with lots of little darting movements. Now it will make quite an arc as it heads for the surface below us.

A fish! Hooked himself, did he? No, I don't think he's big, you have all the pull of the current against you as well as the fish. Try to get him out of the very fast water. Bad luck, he got off. That's a shame, but the current is very strong and the odds favour the fish in these conditions. There's not much you can do about it except to tell yourself that he couldn't have been that big!

Let's examine that fly. After you lose a fish in that manner always have a good look at it. You never know, he may have got off due to the barb being broken – it can happen against a rock or stone – or he may have damaged the hook himself. In either case it would be useless to continue to use the same fly. No, the fly is fine, but it's better to be sure than sorry.

Try the same spot again if you want to, but I think it would be better to move downstream a little and cover some new water. We could move down to point S and have a go at that undercut bank at point L. If I remember rightly you had a nice fish from there the last time we were out.

From here at point S we can easily reach point L, but we have to overcome that fast centre current again. Drag is not the problem this time, our difficulty is to get the fly down deep enough before it is swept away. With the water so high that is quite a deep hole and any fish there is sure to be well down.

I would change that fly for something larger, less stream-lined, something that will really sink quickly. How about a weighted woolly-worm? You may not be familiar with the pattern but try it anyway – we will have a good look at it when we talk about wet flies later.

Before you put on that woolly-worm you had better make an alteration to your leader. That final link of 5 × nylon is totally unsuitable for such a fly. I find that I can manage with the finer tippet most of the time. In fact, I tend to stay with it longer than I should, there are such advantages to fishing fine. However, there comes a time when common sense must prevail, and a fly that has the bulk and weight of a woolly-worm needs a heavier tippet.

The reasons for this are twofold. First, you will find great difficulty in casting such a heavy fly if the tippet is too light. The continuity of movement from the rod tip down the line and leader to the fly is badly impaired. Second, the weight of the fly, during casting, is considerably increased by its speed through the air, and there is the very real risk of it snapping off.

Woolly-worm

Snip off that final link of 5 × nylon where it is tied in at the loop, then substitute a similar length of 3 × nylon. Now you can see the advantage of our type of leader, tippets are changed so easily. We now have 3 × nylon right up to the needle-knot where it joins the braided section, but we still have a loop and knot protecting a break. A knot in nylon considerably reduces its strength and any break that occurs will be at the knot.

Make sure that you thoroughly soak that woolly-worm, and at the same time apply sinkant to the leader. That's right, apply sinkant to all the leader, right up to the line.

You can make a normal back-cast from here, so try to drop the fly just below the inlet and fairly close to the bank.

That's a good cast, just where we wanted it. Quickly, mend the cast upstream to give the fly more time to sink. Good, nicely done. The line is developing a belly downstream, mend upstream again. Good, our fly is still in

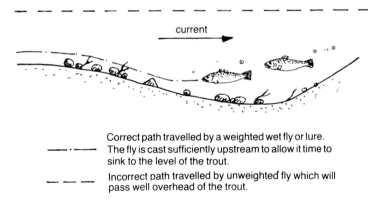

Correct path travelled by a weighted wet fly or lure. The fly is cast sufficiently upstream to allow it time to sink to the level of the trout.

Incorrect path travelled by unweighted fly which will pass well overhead of the trout.

Fig. 16 The hole

The larger fish will often lie deep in depressions or holes. These fish will seldom rise to a fly from this position because a sufficient food supply is carried along the stream bed to them by the current

56

Wading is sometimes very difficult due to many deep holes – but the banks offer ideal cover for the angler working the holes with a deeply sunk woolly worm

the eddy. Nothing doing? Never mind, let the fly continue downstream before you recover it.

There was nothing wrong with that presentation, and I can't believe there are no fish under that bank. Let's try it once again. This time, try to cast a little further upstream so that the fly is swimming deeper by the time it is well into the eddy. Good, mend the line upstream again. Don't watch the mend – watch the tip of the line! Get ready to mend again – *there! Strike!*

Gain control quickly, there is too much line out – good. He's not moving out from the bank, can you still feel him? Are you snagged up? Now he's moving get him away from that bank, it must be full of snags. That's better, I thought we had lost him. A nice fish – he's fighting well. He's off to the bank again, stop him if you can. Now you have him, good firm control, don't let him splash on the surface or we will lose him. Right, I have the net – gently does it – he's ours!

What a lovely fish! Not as big as I thought, but he was certainly a wily character and knew his way around the stream. That undercut bank must be full of snags, the tree roots show even above the water-line. At one stage I was sure we had lost him. Well, he's another one for the bag – it's turning out to be a good day.

I think you were concerned at one stage that your tippet wouldn't take the strain, right? There's no need to worry on that point, 3 × nylon has a breaking strain of approximately $2\frac{3}{4}$ lb (1.3 kg) when it's dry and unknotted. In use, knotted, this is somewhat reduced, perhaps to about $1\frac{1}{2}$ lb (0.7 kg) – it depends on the brand of nylon. However, don't forget that nylon has considerable 'give' and this tends to soften sudden shocks. In addition, you have your rod tip acting as a spring buffer. You must also remember that the fish itself is not a dead weight in the water, in fact it is unable to bring its weight to bear against you. So there is no need to doubt the strength of your leader, always just treat the fish with respect – firmly, but without force – and you shouldn't have any trouble.

I suggest we now move a little downstream. If we go down to point I we may be able to wade out towards point J. I know the water is high, but between I and J the stream bed is fairly level.

Well, we couldn't wade out quite as far as point J. Never mind, we are still in a good position to fish the pool from point H to B.

Do you remember this pool from our last fishing trip? The water was low – about 3 ft (1 m) deep in the centre of the stream – and the stream bed was very uniform. It's a bit different now, at least 8 in (200 mm) deeper and quite coloured. Before, there wasn't a fish to be seen, but now I suspect there are quite a number lying out in the pool. They

The high banks and lack of cover make this kind of river
a difficult water to fish. 'Sweeping' with a wet fly is one
answer to the problem

will feel much safer under these conditions. If we keep to this
side of the stream, I think we will be able to wade without
difficulty.

This type of water requires a rather special technique if
one is to cover it properly. It's a wide and long area, without
any real features, and the fish could be anywhere. The fast
current upstream will bring plenty of food down and the
comparatively slower water here will turn the whole area
into a feeding ground. Under these sorts of conditions I
usually employ a system I call 'sweeping the water'. It can
be done with the minimum of casting and ensures that
practically every foot of water is covered. I will explain it to
you in detail before we start to do anything.

It will help if you take a look at Fig. 17. You let the line
out downstream so that about 15 yd (13.7 m) is extended in
the current (position a). You are then ready to start. The line
is drawn in towards you, position b, by raising the rod tip

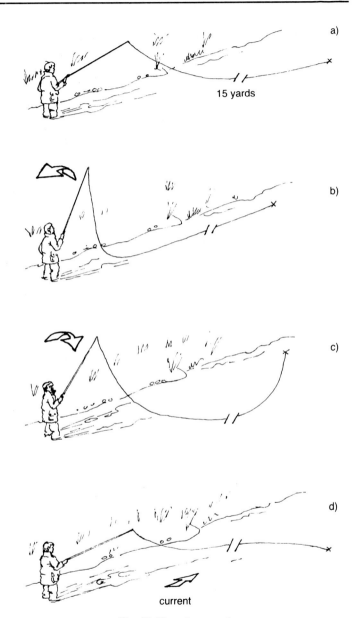

a)

15 yards

b)

c)

d)

current

Fig. 17 'Sweeping a pool'

until a loop of line is hanging down. The rod is then swung over to the right, position c, so that a well-curved line is on the water. Without you doing anything this curve will straighten out in the current and swing the fly to the right. As the fly swings to the right it will rise to the surface in an arc. When the fly has completed its swing to the right it will then swing back towards the left until you are once again in position a.

The line is again drawn towards you, position b, and you repeat the procedure, swinging the rod tip to the left, position d. This time the fly swings to the left in a rising arc.

Once you have swept both the left- and right-hand sides in front of you, it is time to wade forward a couple of paces and repeat the whole procedure again. In this way you continue down the full length of the pool. Now you can see what I mean by 'sweeping the water' with the minimum of casting. Have you got the idea?

In this type of operation the fly basically becomes a nymph rising to the surface. A fly worked this way will often raise a number of smaller fish, but with the water high and coloured I am hopeful that larger fish are present and will arrive there first. We will have to see.

Before we start, change the tippet back to 5 × nylon and dry the whole leader with a piece of rag. Now we can grease the braided portion so that it will float, and treat the tippet portion with sinkant. We don't want to fish deep here – a couple of feet down will do nicely.

I will let you have one of my favourite 'sweeping' flies. I have never given it a name, I suppose it's really a nymph that has been tied to reflect the light. Let's call it a 'reflector nymph', I will tell you all about it later.

Ready to start? Right, let's start 'sweeping the pool'.

You are doing well. It's necessary to watch your leader for a take as it begins to swing, but once the swing is well under way, and the fly is rising, a take can be easily felt on the line.

61

Always the question – and worth thinking through to the
answer: 'Which fly? They have seen everything in my box –
except the bit of fluff in the corner!'

A fish taking a rising fly invariably hooks himself as he turns
back down.

I'm surprised we haven't taken a fish by now. We've
covered quite a lot of the pool and you're working that
'sweep' very well. Perhaps we will do better when – *a fish!*
Well done, you obviously felt the draw on the line.

Try not to give any line, we don't want to disturb where
we haven't yet fished. That's right, draw him over to this
side. Gently, remember how easily they get off the hook
when they fight downstream. That's fine – I don't think you
will want the net, he's only about $\frac{1}{2}$ lb (0.2 kg). You think he's
more than that? You may be right, he's lively enough. If you
are not going to keep him, try to make the release in the
water. Run your fingers down the leader and try to shake
him off the fly. He's away, good.

Sometimes that works very well, and although it shakes them up a bit, I'm sure it's much better than handling them. I bet it will be a couple of days before he goes back on the feed!

Did the feel of that take surprise you? Yes, it very often is quite a tug. For some reason they seem to react quite savagely to a rising fly. Perhaps they think it is on the way to the surface to hatch and will escape from them. You must be very careful not to be startled into reacting too sharply and tugging back just as hard. If you do that, the hook nearly always tears out. Just tighten on them to set the hook well – no hard strike is required.

Carry on 'sweeping', we may catch his big brother! Now is the time to be really attentive. We are starting to fish in the tail of the pool and this is always a gathering point for the fish. Any fish we take near points A, B or C are very dangerously close to those rocks and the fast water below. Once

The wide expanses of shallow broken water indicate to the angler the presence of a rocky stream bed – perfect lies for feeding trout

into the rocks and fast water and they will be lost to us.

Another take! Hold him – he's into the rocks! Well done, back in the pool. Look at him go! You have a good one there, you will have to give line a little – you can't be too rough with him while he is below you. That's the second time he's taken off, but you should have him now if the hook holds. Good, he's coming in. Pass me the net – gently over it – we have him!

He's no bigger than the ones you already have, but he's a very nice fish. Doesn't the strength of them surprise you? They are so beautifully fit. Look at the colour – they're so handsome! Do you want to keep him? Let's put him back, you have a good brace and it's a shame to take more than that. I'm glad you agree – he's off! I didn't even see him go, they are so fast in the water.

Well, it's been a good day. You can't ask for more. It won't do us any good to fish in this pool until it settles down again, and that will take quite a time. Shall we call it a day? When we get home we can talk about wet flies.

CHAPTER 7

WET FLIES

Wet flies were in use a very long time before the appearance of the dry fly, and many of the early patterns are still in use today. To these earlier patterns so many others have been added that the choice today is vast. It is almost impossible to think of a colour combination, or a combination of materials, that has not already been used.

A study of these numerous patterns results in the realisation that very little has been done to imitate natural insect-life – nearly all patterns are designed purely to attract. It would seem that the theory is that if one combination of colours will not attract, another will. Quite a number of these flies have been named for particular insects, but this is mostly due to the colours used and has very little to do with any attempt at imitation.

All this leads to the question, why do trout take these flies? We don't know, and that's the root of the problem. If we knew the answer we would be able to design new and better wet flies, instead of which the so-called 'new, wet flies' are nothing more than the old combinations re-hashed into different permutations.

Attempts have been made to design a different type of wet fly that imitates the natural nymph. You will notice that I refer to the results of these attempts as a 'type of wet fly'.

Well, at the risk of making a lot of enemies, that's how I see them – and not only because they are used wet and below the surface. These attempts at imitation of natural nymphs are no better than those we see trying to imitate the hatched fly. Nothing created by man out of fly-tying materials can in any way closely resemble the natural nymph.

Mind you, we have said all this before about dry flies, and were forced to the conclusion that if they take fish, then something about them must delude the fish. We can be certain of one thing – they are not taken because they so closely resemble the natural insect that the fish can't tell the difference.

It would be easy at this point to return to the theory that these flies create an illusion of the natural insect, which itself is not that clear, and consequently the illusion is a very good imitation of what the trout normally expects to see. This theory might be acceptable in the case of the dry fly seen through two mediums – water and air – but the wet fly is a different matter: it is in the trout's own medium, clearly in his view. It is amazing how often, in this type of discussion, one comes full circle without finding an answer. Why do the trout take these artificials? I only wish we knew!

I have long thought that the reason a trout takes a wet fly is possibly different each time it is taken, depending entirely on what movement the fly was making at that time. Obviously the fly is taken as food and, depending on its behaviour at the very moment it is taken, is the type of food it is believed to be by the trout.

A wet fly on a free drift downstream could, perhaps, be taken as a drowned land-blown insect, as a drowned, aquatic fly, as a free-swimming nymph, or as a slow-moving small fish-fry. A wet fly that is being made to dart about could be confused with a darting nymph, or more likely with a small fish-fry. When the wet fly is rising to the surface in a sweeping arc, it is probably taken as a nymph rising to the surface to hatch but it could also be taken as a fast moving fish-fry. There are also many other subaquatic creatures that have to rise to the surface periodically to breathe air.

So perhaps the multi-colours and the tinsel ribbing of these flies do serve a purpose, even if we are not fully aware of what that purpose is. Under the various conditions they are seen by the trout along with their varied motions through the water, perhaps at a particular instant in time they truly represent what the trout imagines them to be.

What about artificial nymphs? Do they represent nymphs more truly than standard wet flies? They certainly catch fish, of that there is no doubt, but do they enhance your chance of a fish, or do they reduce your chance? If they truly imitate natural nymphs it follows that they must reduce your chance by failing to represent any other form of food. However, they do not pass inspection as true imitations of natural nymphs. Consequently, they may well be taken as a completely different food form.

I am left with the feeling that the 'nymph' may well become a cult in the same way that the dry fly became a cult in the late nineteenth century. This is somewhat borne out by the insistence that its correct use is 'upstream'. Why? What difference does it make if the nymph is travelling in a free drift downstream towards the angler, or downstream in a free drift away from the angler? I assume that on rivers where upstream dry fly is the general rule, the presentation of the nymph has followed the same ruling. This is borne out by the fact that, in the main, these same rivers have a rule forbidding the use of wet flies downstream.

These rules have no place on our type of stream where we fish the fly in the way it is most productive. Use artificial nymphs by all means – they are good takers of fish – but do not look upon them as the answer to all your problems. Under general conditions they may well have a reverse effect and you would be better off using a standard wet fly.

Another vexing question is how many wet flies to a cast? Many years ago it was standard procedure to use multiple flies tied on droppers standing out from the cast. In fact, this is still very much accepted practice on Scottish and Irish still waters. Many reservoir anglers adopt the same procedure with quite good results. On a small stream I have always found that the disadvantages are so great that the multiple system is not worth while. We have enough bankside and overhead vegetation to overcome – to say nothing of underwater snags – without giving ourselves further items to snag up. It's a matter of individual choice – I prefer to stay with the single fly.

When it comes to choosing a selection of wet flies for your fly box, I can only offer general advice. Many of the patterns have, over the years, become household names and are proven killers of fish. This applies mostly to the older patterns that were specifically designed for river use, or to the traditional loch patterns. Although the loch patterns will take fish in a stream, I find that they are most useful when their use is confined to high and coloured water, and when they are tied on much smaller hooks than is the usual loch practice.

There are so many wet flies to choose from, representing multiple food forms, that I would suggest a good initial selection could be made by giving standard river patterns first choice, and only taking still-water patterns if they are sparsely dressed and on hooks smaller than size 12.

Nymphs? That is up to you. Yes, put a few in your box by all means, they can always be tried when the going is extra tough. At times they have brought me fish when all else has failed. However, try to remember that they are not the final answer and keep an open mind. The following list may be helpful:

Standard low-water river patterns

Gold-ribbed hare's-ear	Hook size	14 and 16
March brown	Hook size	14 and 16
Lead-winged coachman	Hook size	14 and 16
Greenwell's glory	Hook size	14 and 16
Wickman's fancy	Hook size	14 and 16
Reflector nymph	Hook size	16 and 18
Woolly-worm	Hook size	14 long shank

Still-water patterns (of limited use in high and coloured water)

Mallard and claret	Hook size	12 and 14
Invictor	Hook size	12 and 14
Teal and silver	Hook size	12 and 14
Peter Ross	Hook size	12 and 14
Alexander	Hook size	12 and 14

While we were fishing we used a woolly-worm. This particular pattern is very old, perhaps among the first wet flies ever used. Not under the name of 'woolly-worm', and certainly not tied like the one we used, the general pattern was in use among the first anglers to fish with a fly.

Without doubt it was originally designed to be fished wet, but some years ago it found its way to the USA and for some unknown reason was redesigned as a dry fly and given the name 'woolly-worm'. In the USA the name 'woolly-worm' is given to those black, hairy caterpillars with the orange underside. I believe they are the caterpillar of one of the moths. The woolly-worm is used to imitate those caterpillars that fall, or are blown, upon the water. In the USA it is tied with black deer-hair spun onto the hook shank (muddler-minnow style). The hair is then clipped close and the underside painted orange. The fly is finished off with a black hackle tied palmer.

14 long shank

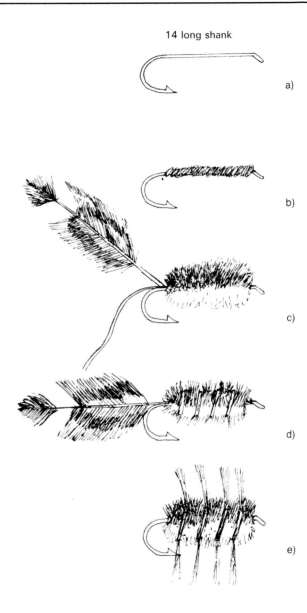

a)

b)

c)

d)

e)

Fig. 18 The woolly-worm

Tied in this manner the fly is a very good floater – in fact it is almost impossible to sink. I have used it many times in this form and have at times taken fish, but the results were far from spectacular.

After discussions with several angling friends it was decided to revert the fly to its original role – a wet fly – but to keep the American colours and name. The result was the woolly-worm we used while we were fishing – designed to represent a drowned land-blown insect.

If you look at Fig. 18, the stages in construction will be easily followed. The hook, usually a size-14 long shank, is bent to the shape shown at (a). After whipping down the shank with tying-silk (black) in the usual way, copper wire is added to give the weighting required (b). A black hackle and a length of flat, silver tinsel tied in at the bend is shown in (c). The body is then wound with black chenille (fine grade) and tied off at the head. At this stage the fly is turned over in the vice and the underside painted with orange, cellulose varnish.

The fly must be absolutely dry before continuing the dressing; (d) shows the silver tinsel wound as a rib. Finally, (e) shows the finished fly with the hackle wound palmer. The head is kept as small as possible and finished off with black varnish. We have all had considerably better results with the

Fig. 19 The reflector nymph

Hook: 14 or 16 long shank
Body: Flat, gold tinsel, ribbed with fine, oval, gold tinsel – very well lacquered
Tail: Few fibres of grizzle hackle tied in long
Wing: Grizzle-hackle fibres – tied in very short

Reflector nymph

woolly-worm tied this way. I know of nothing better for fishing those deep holes – at least, nothing better that is artificial!

The reflector nymph (see Fig. 19) was never really designed by anyone. It owes its origin to some obscure wet fly – I can't remember which – that was in my fly box when I needed a gold-tinsel-bodied fly in coloured water. Much later I formed the opinion that such a fly with a gold-tinsel body, having good reflecting qualities, might well reflect the brown rocks and stones of the stream bed when fished in clear water. In this way the brown translucence of the natural nymph might be imitated.

It seemed a natural progression to clip back the regular wing so that the outline more closely resembled the natural nymph's wing-cases. Then, having little faith that it truly imitated any natural nymph, it was relegated to the bottom of my fly box.

When I started using the 'sweeping' technique, with the emphasis on the rising wet fly, attention was, once again, directed towards the fly with the gold-tinsel body. More flies were tied, this time with the body of gold tinsel also ribbed with oval, gold tinsel for increased reflection. In addition the finished bodies were treated to several coats of clear, cellulose varnish. As the intention was to create a nymph-like outline, the clipped-back wing was retained and a long tail added.

I am still far from convinced that the fly is a good nymph imitation, but I feel reasonably sure that the reflective qualities do give a brown–amber translucence that is not out of keeping with natural insects. The clipped wing and long tail may, or may not, complete the illusion.

The results have been excellent. Wild brownies, which are not usually inclined towards bright flies, have shown little hesitation in taking this fly, even in clear water. It is now one of the flies that I regularly use, and is my first choice for 'sweeping' a pool. I hope it may be equally productive for others using the same technique.

One summer evening eleven brownies were taken from this beautiful pool in South Wales – all on a reflector nymph

Most wet-fly patterns call for wings made from feather fibre. There is little motion possible from such material, and the wing is inclined to retain its shape and outline. I have long considered that motion is a distinct advantage as it varies the outline of the fly when it moves through the water. The best way to achieve this movement is to tie wings made from the rolled fibres of such feathers as mallard, teal, grouse or partridge. The fibres, if cut from the centre stalk, can be rolled together then tied in as a bunch, making sure to keep the wing on the sparse side.

Whenever tying, or purchasing, wet flies, the aim should always be to obtain flies that have a 'streamlined' appearance. The purpose of this is to achieve a clean and fast entry when they land on the water so that they sink subsurface without delay. Nothing is worse than a wet fly that insists on floating. If your fly will not sink even after repeated soaking, the problem is probably caused by the fly being 'over-dressed'. A little careful work with the scissors thinning down the hackle, etc., will help matters considerably – and produce a better fly.

The next time we are together we should talk about the use of midge and non-aquatic insect patterns. They are an important part of the trout's diet and we can't afford to ignore them.

CHAPTER 8

FISHING TACTICS
(3)

Although midges and non-aquatic insects form such an important part of a trout's diet, it is almost impossible to arrange a fishing trip based solely on the use of artificials to imitate these insects.

Not only do conditions for their use have to be just right, but also the time of the day must be taken into account. During the summer months, especially late summer when fly

An ideal water for fishing dry fly and terrestrials

hatches are inclined to become sparse, the trout turn more to opportunist feeding. The period at dusk may or may not bring out an abundance of midges – it depends on the temperature during the day and the pressure system of the weather. The fall of beetles, ants, caterpillars, etc., upon the water depends so much on the wind – not only the strength of the wind but also its direction.

In consequence, we must be prepared at all times to use these artificials as and when the occasion demands. They are a very necessary and vital addition to our fly box. However, we cannot decide on a particular day to fish these artificials to the exclusion of all other flies, it would almost certainly result in a poor day's sport.

It is better that we sit and talk about these insects. I can show you the contents of my fly box and describe the way these artificials should be used. We can even reminisce a little – there have been many occasions when these special flies have given me memorable days to look back on.

The first fly we should discuss is the midge. I find that very few anglers have a clear idea of what an artificial midge should look like, and even less idea on how or when it should be used. The artificial midge is *not* a very small, dry fly. So often you see small dry flies that have been dressed on minute hooks and are offered for sale as 'midges'. In most cases the fly itself is dressed out of all proportion to the hook size, sometimes to the point of destroying its hooking capabilities. There is little purpose in tying what should have been a size-16 fly on a hook that is, perhaps, size 20 – it is still a size-16 fly! Besides, an artificial only just qualifies for the midge class when it is size 20!

When we speak of midges we are referring to that multitude of small flies that at times hovers over water, sometimes lightly touching it in its gyrations, at other times getting caught in the surface film. Some of these insects are aquatic flies that hatch from the water; others are land-based insects attracted by the humidity and the bankside vegetation. Identification is extremely difficult due to their minute size. One thing they have in common is that they are all very *small*. So small, in fact, that imitation is an impossibility.

However, we do have one thing in our favour. When the trout are feeding on midges, the insects they take are not always the same species, colour or size. Although the trout may be classed as feeding selectively, he is only selective because the bulk of the food on offer is small sized – he is not often particular as to which midge he takes. To satisfy this criterion we only need to use small flies – and it is at this point that our difficulties commence!

Let us get it clearly established in our minds, we are talking of flies that are tied as small as it is humanly possible to tie them. We are talking about hooks that are size 20, 22 or 24! Smaller hooks can sometimes be obtained but the tying of such flies is almost impossible.

We are fortunate that today these small hooks are of excellent quality, beautifully tempered and formed. However, most of them are not nearly sharp enough and the points require a little treatment before use. I find that the average stone, or hone, is of little use on hooks this size. It is better to use the point of an H-grade pencil.

The form of a midge artificial should be as shown in Fig. 20(a), *not* as shown in Fig. 20(b). The colour of the fly is not that important: I find that black, brown and white will cover most situations. They have no body except the tying-silk, which should be the same colour as the hackle – except in the case of the white midge when olive silk is preferable.

Tying so simple a fly is not difficult, even in such a small size, but obtaining hackles of the right size is another matter. Unless you are very lucky and have such hackles, you will have to use the smallest you have and trim them to shape with sharp scissors. It is very much better to have a trimmed

a)   b)

Fig. 20 The miniature fly
(a) The midge
(b) The over-dressed fly

fly of the correct shape than to leave the hackle over size.

One thing must always be remembered when deciding to use a midge fly: the leader must be altered to suit the fly. To cast these flies properly it is essential that the tippet is reduced to 6 × or 7 × nylon. Our normal tippet of 5 × nylon cannot be exchanged for a length of 6 × or 7 × as this would mean that the new length would be knotted directly to 3 × nylon – far too big a step down. We must add the new length to our existing tippet and fish with a 9–10-ft (2.7–3-m) leader.

Fishing with a tippet as fine as 6 × or 7 × nylon needs special care. If the nylon is of good quality and carefully knotted you should still have a breaking strain of over $\frac{1}{2}$ lb (0.2 kg), but keep a very careful eye on the tippet for wind-knots: they will reduce your breaking strain to almost zero. Also, when playing a fish, keep your rod tip low and pointing in the direction of the fish. I know that this is contrary to all you have been taught, but these super-light tippets are an exception and rod-ring friction must be reduced.

I remember some years ago I was staying at a fishing lodge on the Beaverkill River in the Catskill Mountains of Upper New York State. This river has the reputation of being one of the premier streams of the area – it certainly holds some superb trout. It's a 'fly-only' water of superlative quality, and the fish are wild and wary.

One morning, as I walked along the bank, I saw a beautiful brown trout steadily rising in the head of a pool. It was a very deep pool, much too deep to see the bed of the stream and the water had a lovely, clear, greenish hue. The trout was magnificent, golden and heavily spotted. As he rose to take each fly his gills extended so that his head appeared to enlarge. He was every bit of 5 lb (2.3 kg). I was fascinated by his regular rising. He was lying about 18 in (0.5 m) from where the fast water tumbled into the pool and obviously had the total food supply to himself.

When I returned to the lodge after my walk I was full of the trout I had seen and told everyone there about it. I was surprised at the reaction of my fellow anglers. They all appeared to know of this fish and showed very little interest. It seemed that this trout made a regular habit of rising at that particular spot and nearly everyone, at one time or another, had had a try for him – obviously without success. The general consensus of opinion was that if one fished an artificial to him, he just didn't take. He hadn't grown to 5 lb (2.3 kg) in the Beaverkill by being stupid!

I was determined to try a different approach. The next day I made my way up to the pool from well downstream. The water shelved away into the pool quite sharply from shallow water along the opposite bank, and I was able to wade quite easily in 2 ft (0.6 m) of water until I was within casting distance.

I stood very quietly and waited. There was no sign of the fish I was after, but I was sure he was there. It was warm and sunny and I was soon surrounded by midges – and in that part of the world they bite! I lighted my pipe and continued my wait, blowing out clouds of smoke. After what seemed a very long time I saw a rise, followed by another, then another. He was back on station!

I started to fish for him. I was using my standard 5 × tippet, and I cast carefully into the fast water just as it entered the pool. I was certain that my fly was passing directly over him, and equally certain that he hadn't seen the cast – just the fly washed to him by the fast water. However, nothing. That is, nothing happened until my fly had passed over, then he rose to the next natural that came along!

After all these years I can't remember how many times I changed flies: it must have been five or six times. The result was the same each time, after my fly passed over he rose to the next natural.

I stopped casting in order to have a rest and to think matters out. Obviously my quiet approach had worked: I had been able to cast continuously to him without disturbing his routine, but it wasn't getting me anywhere at all. True, I could congratulate myself on my stealth, on the delicate casting and the fineness of the tackle, but the object was to catch fish!

Standing quietly in the stream I lengthened my leader by adding a length of the finest nylon in my pocket – probably 6 × – then selected a size-22 midge. I didn't bother to try to make the leader sink, whatever you do to 6 × nylon it always seems to float in the surface film. However, I did soak the fly in floatant and give it time to dry off. I couldn't take the risk of too many false-casts.

My first cast placed the midge onto the fast water. I was completely unable to see the fly or leader but knew from the direction of my flyline where it was. Now the fly must be in the pool. *A rise!* It must be to my fly. *Strike!*

There was quite a swirl on the surface, then nothing. Either my strike had been premature or he had taken and ejected before I could connect.

I could do nothing but wait to see if he would rise again.

80

I waited a long time; I stood there so quietly and so long that I saw several good-size trout take up position in my shadow – less than 3 ft (1 m) away! He didn't rise again.

I left the lodge the next day and have never had the opportunity to return. I sincerely hope that beautiful trout saw out his natural life in that pool until he succumbed to old age.

I suppose you could call that encounter a dismal failure, particularly if you consider success only in the light of fish caught. However, to me it was not a failure: no encounter with a trout is a complete failure if we learn something as a result. I had been given to understand that this trout would not take an artificial, and my earlier attempts to raise him bore this out. However, even a cagey old trout, stream bred, and fully aware of angler's ways, was able to be tempted by a minute midge presented on a super-fine tippet. Could I have held him if my strike had connected? I will never know – but I would have had a good try!

We should now consider other food forms that interest trout. Let me show you some artificials from my fly box that do not have any connection with aquatic flies – they represent land-blown insects, or terrestrials, as they are sometimes called. They form a substantial part of the food taken by trout in the mid-season. To fish mid-season successfully, the so-called 'dog days', you must seriously consider the use of terrestrials.

Trout do not take up a feeding station to gorge on these insects – only the odd tasty morsel comes their way – but when it does they take it! During the warmer, sultry days, trout are inclined to lie motionless in the shadier parts of the stream, under deep banks, under over-hanging vegetation, and especially close into banks that are undercut: all very good and likely places for them to encounter terrestrials.

The types of land-blown insects that find themselves on the water are many, and in the majority of cases the trout are

81

Heavily wooded streams provide opportunities to fish terrestrials throughout the summer months

not particular. Grasshoppers, beetles, caterpillars, ants, etc.,
are all tasty morsels; so are moths, horse-flies and wasps. I
have never found a satisfactory imitation as far as grasshoppers are concerned, which is a pity for they are the most
sought after. The problem with the grasshopper is that it
makes violent movements when it finds itself on the water
and there is no satisfactory way to imitate them. Beetles are
a different matter: they are inclined to float motionless with
their wings extended beyond their wing-cases. A fair
imitation can be tied, see Fig. 21.

The dressing of the beetle in Fig. 21 is as follows:

Hook:	14 long shank.
Underbody:	Padded with black floss.
Legs:	Black hackle wound palmer and the top half clipped.

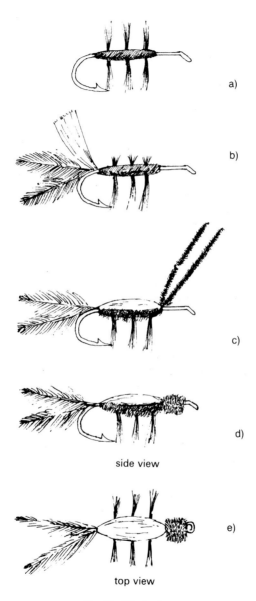

side view

top view

Fig. 21 The beetle

Tail:	Two, small, ginger hackles, the length of the hook shank.
Overbody:	Wide strip of pheasant tail, well lacquered after tying down.
Head:	Green, peacock harl.

The illustrations (a) to (e) in Fig. 21 are self-explanatory. However, a few tips may be useful. When padding the underbody it should be made quite fat so as to support the overbody. The palmer hackle needs to be well clipped so that only the bottom half remains. This can be left quite sparse as it is only intended to represent legs. The overbody is laid over the top as flat as possible, then given several coats of clear, cellulose varnish, allowing it to dry thoroughly between coats. When tying in the extended wings they should be slightly overlapped and tied in so that they will lie flat on the water.

The artificial beetle fished with a dead drift very close to the bank can be a deadly lure to a basking trout. Perhaps its use can be best described by the following incident.

I had obtained a day ticket to fish the upper reaches of the Teifi River in mid-Wales. The river was new to me at that time but I had high hopes of a good day: the upper reaches have an excellent reputation for brown trout. The day I was on the water it was early summer, but it was very warm and bright – one of those rare, early, sultry days.

I worked my way upstream using a variety of dry flies, but with very little success. It is a river of constantly-changing currents: the underwater plant-life is prolific in places and the water flow is in one place restricted, in another it speeds its way through channels between the weed beds. Consequently, drag on the fly was a constant problem. Wading was a further problem as even in summer this river runs quite deep. It seemed that I had no sooner found a wadable stretch when I would be forced out of the water by the depth.

Working terrestrials under the over-hanging branches.
Difficult to perfect but worth-while in the end

Although the banks were over-grown in places, there were
long stretches where bank fishing was possible. I am never
happy dry-fly fishing from a high bank. Even keeping low I
still feel very exposed to the fish. Also, a good presentation
downwards to the water is rather difficult.

After taking one medium-sized trout on the dry fly I
decided to change over to the wet fly. Things started to
improve. By carefully working the channels between the
weed beds I was able to take a number of trout, none of them
large but all nice fish.

Having taken seven fish I was satisfied with my day. I had
not encountered any of the large brownies that the water was
reputed to hold, but not knowing the water I felt I had
nothing to complain about. I began the long walk along the
bank to the bridge where I had left the car.

At one point along the bank I had to push my way
through quite dense bushes. For some yards the river was

hidden from view down a very steep bank. As I made my way I heard a distinct loud 'plop' from the water. Every flyfisher knows that sound – it could only mean the slow, determined rise of a large fish!

I gently pushed my way through the bushes until I could see the water. It was a lovely pool, deep with a gentle current, and there were no weed beds in the vicinity. There was no sign of any movement or of any fish, but I couldn't see under the bank on which I was standing. I waited patiently to see if the rise would be repeated. Suddenly the 'plop' sounded again but it was right under the overhanging bank and quite invisible to me.

Having decided to go after the fish, I made my way along the bank upstream until I found a break in the bushes. Fortunately this was within casting distance and I was able to climb down the bank to the water – but it was far too deep to wade out into the stream to cast.

What was I to do? It was obvious that this trout was feeding close to the bank on something or other off the land. I decided on a beetle that could be floated down to him on a dead drift.

I didn't really cast at all, I just flicked out a short line very close to the bank and paid out line by stripping it off the reel and twitching it through the rod rings. Away went the beetle downstream, out of sight under the over-hanging branches. After it had travelled a distance, I saw the line give a definite twitch. I'd felt nothing, but I gave a hard strike anyway. I had him! The best fish of the day! Yes, the beetle can be a deadly lure under the right conditions.

Another insect that has always fascinated me is the ant. They come in such a variety of sizes and colours. To the trout, regardless of size or colour, they just represent food and are taken in enormous quantities. Sometimes the source of food is obvious when a few, large, carpenter ants have been blown onto the water; at other times the sipping rises give no indication unless one studies the surface film very closely. There is no doubt that literally thousands of ants find their way onto the water.

There are many patterns of imitation ants, both large and small. Over a long period I have added many of my own, some even coloured red and yellow! I'm afraid I have never had any real success with any of these patterns. True, I have taken trout on imitation ants, but they have been few and far between. I have heard of much better results by other anglers, so perhaps I have a jinx as far as the ant is concerned. I would not decry their use – by all means have a try for yourself – perhaps the answer lies with the large-winged ant fished as a dry fly, or perhaps with the very small, red variety tied on a midge hook. I will certainly continue with my efforts, I refuse to be beaten by an ant!

Flies of the wasp family, although rare on the water, are always greedily taken by the trout whenever they are available. The best pattern I know is one from the USA called a 'McGinty' (see Fig. 22). Although this fly is to all appearances a dry fly, it always fished semi-submerged in the

Fig. 22 The 'McGinty'
Hook: 12 dry fly
Body: Two lengths of fine chenille, one black, one yellow, tied in together and wound alternatively
Hackle: Ginger-cock hackle
Head: Black and large

'McGinty'

surface film. To achieve this effect the fly is never treated with floatant: the chenille body takes up water but the hackle stops it from sinking completely below the surface. It is fished upstream as a dry fly.

The 'McGinty' is a first-class fly for a hot, bright, summer's day. It can be cast to all likely shady spots when nothing else seems to be on the water and no fish appear to be moving. Sometimes the results are fantastic.

Another favourite terrestrial of mine is the green caterpillar – I'm never without one or two in my fly box (see Fig. 23). This simple pattern has caught many fish for me, and seems irresistible to the trout. In life they are very lively and if touched will wriggle in all directions as if trying to tie themselves in a knot. However, once on the water they become lifeless and lie on the surface stretched out straight.

Fig. 23 The green caterpillar
Hook: 14 long shank
Body: Fine green chenille, wound in touching turns
Head: Bronze-peacock harl

Some years ago I was a member of a Canadian fishing
syndicate in Ontario. We called our water 'Rainbow
Ranch', which was a fair description as the majority of fish
in the water were rainbow trout. The water consisted of
several small lakes fed from small streams. Some of the lakes
had connecting streams. To improve the fish population,
large breeders were netted out at the appropriate time,
stripped of eggs and milt, then returned to the water. The

Green caterpillar

89

fry were reared separately until they were fingerlings, then placed in the various lakes. In this way the fish population was assured and the fishing was excellent.

Yes, the fishing was excellent, but very far from easy. The fish were wild and wily, not a bit like the 'stockies' from pellet-fed stew-ponds. The lakes themselves were rich in food and the fish grew well – a 4-lb (1.8-kg) fish was considered to be medium size!

Dry-fly fishing was the procedure for the streams, sometimes on the lakes as well. In Ontario the spring and autumn seasons can be very cold – ice in the rod rings – and then it was wet flies most of the time. It was the high summer that brought us our most difficult time, normally very hot and humid with the fish almost dormant. A day's fishing in mid-summer was classified as an enormous success if it resulted in more than one fish.

One particularly hot day, it must have been in the upper eighties, we were all fishless and taking it easy under a few shady trees. We suddenly noticed a lot of surface activity under the trees further along the bank – there were so many rises that the water appeared to be boiling. Investigations soon revealed the reason. The trees were literally full of green caterpillars and large numbers were falling onto the water below.

Various patterns were tried with differing results. I was in the fortunate position of having several green-caterpillar imitations in my fly box – in Canada it is called an 'inch worm'.

I won't bore you with details of the fishing, just to say that the imitation caterpillar was not worked in the water in any way, it was cast out then left to lie on the surface. The end result of my day's fishing was a total of eighteen fish, not one of them under 2 lb (0.9 kg)! Have no doubts about it – the green caterpillar, or 'inch worm', deserves a place in your fly box.

White moth

Lastly we must not forget the common moth, which must also be classified as a terrestrial as it is a land insect and has no connection with the water. They are nocturnal insects but they do commence their activities at dusk, which is of considerable help to us. For some reason they are attracted by the surface of the water – probably because of light reflection – and their flight often takes them down to the surface. Once on the water they become very active and are quite capable of taking off and resuming their flight. Very often they skitter across the surface in their attempts to become airborne again.

Without doubt they are very attractive to trout, and are taken whenever the opportunity presents itself. Their action on the water is not unlike those of the sedge fly and both flies are the cause of the slashing rises that result from the trout taking them as the flies attempt to become airborne.

I know of no better pattern to imitate the moth than that

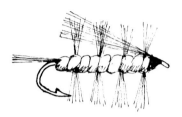

Fig. 24 The great white moth
Hook: 12 long shank
Body: Medium white chenille
Hackle: White-cock hackle, wound palmer
Wing: White swan-feather fibres, trimmed to length and cut off square
Tail: White swan-feather fibres, tied very short

devised by the late Dick Walker (see Fig. 24). Fished as a dry
fly at dusk, it can be very effective. After dark – if you insist
on night fishing – it is better if the fly is dressed completely
black. No matter how dark it becomes, the sky is always
brighter than the water below the surface. Looking up,
without the benefit of side lighting, the trout always see flies
at night in silhouette. The darker the fly the more intense is
the silhouette.

When using the moth pattern it is not necessary, within
reason, to worry about drag. If the fly is well treated with
floatant the drag may well skitter it over the surface, which
is exactly what we are after. In practice I have often found
that it is at the moment of drag that the fly is most often
taken. One of the best trout that it has been my pleasure to
land took one of these flies as I was reeling in to end my day's
fishing!

I hope you are convinced of the value of midges and
'terrestrials', and will stock up your fly box accordingly. The
next time we go fishing it will be early season – the best time
to use 'streamerettes'.

CHAPTER 9

FISHING TACTICS

(4)

When I said earlier that I hoped we would have the opportunity to fish together at the start of the season, I had overlooked how cold the early season can be. It's nice to be out together again, but we couldn't have picked a colder day! That cold north-easterly wind is not much help either, although at this time of the year it's to be expected.

I thought we might go to a small stream near the South Wales coast. During the summer months the water in this stream is little better than a series of riffles between the deeper holes. At this time of the year the flow will be much better and the holes deeper – it should give us a good opportunity to try out different tactics.

If you look at the plan of the stream (see Fig. 25), you will see that a small bridge crosses the stream. We will park the car near the bridge and start operations from there.

To enjoy fishing on a day like this it is essential to be properly dressed: a day can be so easily spoiled by lack of forethought. Several layers of light clothing are much better than one, heavy, woollen sweater, and I find that a pair of thermal socks – at least knee length – are essential if you are intending to wade. It is a definite fact that if your head is cold you feel cold all over, so a warm hat is also necessary. A wind-proof fishing jacket, the waxed-cotton type is best, and

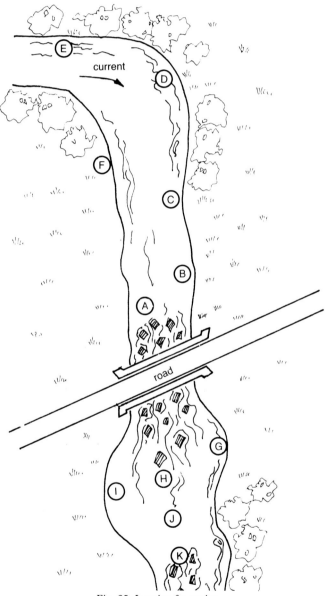

current

road

Fig. 25 Location for tactics

it will help maintain body warmth. For years I have always used a pair of game-shooter's mittens at this time of the year, they have non-slip palms and don't soak up any water.

Before we commence fishing we will have to make an alteration to our leader. We will do the same as when we fished the heavy woolly-worm, we will dispense with the extra-fine tippet and add a 24-in (0.6-m) length of 3 × material instead. We are going to use a streamerette, and although the fly is not particularly heavy it is larger than we generally use. It will need the extra tippet thickness to be cast properly.

Let me show you a streamerette. I agree that it's an unusual shape, but at this time of the year they can be very effective. We will talk about them in detail when we are back in the warm later on.

The whole purpose of the streamerette is to fish the deeper holes and pools. It will be fished in the same manner as a bait fisher uses a small minnow. The fish are now lean and hungry and are looking for something substantial. Most of the larger fish are now down deep where the water is warmer.

Let's walk along the bank, upstream, to point E. There is a good hole at point D that might hold a fish or two. The water at point E is not deep, so we will be able to enter the water quietly to give ourselves room to cast. You can see that the bend in the stream has created a minor pool with a deep hole under that far bank. There is a definite water flow but it is steady rather than fast. In this type of fishing we ignore the direction of the current, except where it helps us to get the fly down deep to where the fish may be lying.

When we fish the streamerette it must never be just carried by the current, it must be constantly on the move. We must impart a constant darting action to it by manipulating the line with our left hand and at the same time moving our rod tip – a similar routine to the way we made our wet flies work, but this time we will also be retrieving across the current as well.

Right, let's make our first cast, a short one, to just above point D. Good, now start paying out line by stripping it from the reel and passing it through the rod rings by waggling your rod tip from side to side. As the current takes the fly downstream there will be movement of the fly, and all the time the fly is sinking deeper. Now that the fly is into the pool start to retrieve by short, sharp pulls on the line. Every few pulls give a pause to let the fly sink back with the current, then carry out the same retrieve again. It's a 'sink-and-draw' type of retrieve that we want to achieve. You are doing fine. As you retrieve vary the lengths of the pulls. That's good, you are getting a nice darting action with a 'sink-back' in between. Carry on that way. When you have retrieved enough line you will be in a position to cast again.

If you feel that the fly needs to swim a little deeper, then delay the retrieve for a while, but keep the fly moving by jiggling your rod tip.

You will soon know if the fly is taken – in most cases the take is quite savage. Obviously we are trying to imitate the movements of a small bait-fish. If we successfully do this the take will be a savage attack. Brown trout normally hit their prey at the head end, and hit very hard. An instantaneous strike-back could well cause a break. On the other hand, you will need to set the hook, which may not have taken a good hold. Whenever I can, I try to exercise enough self-control just to tighten as soon as I feel a take, then a split second later I strike back hard to set the hook. Much easier said than done!

That cast seems to be working out well, the fly is quite deep down in the pool. Keep it working with short, sharp, little pulls. That's right, keep moving the rod tip at the same time. It really is cold work on a day like – *you're into a fish!*

Keep a tight line! Did you strike back? He's a good one,

I bet you felt that take! Let him take a little line if he wants to, but make sure he has no slack. I can see him now, nice and steady does it – I have the net ready – draw him over it. Well done! He's a nice-size fish, but look how lean he is, he must have been really hungry. Let's put him back – we'll catch him again later on in the season when he's good and fat!

You say the take was quite a pull? I expect it was. It always comes as a surprise, no matter how much you anticipate it. One moment you are working the fly, the next you are into a fish!

Although we normally think of early season as the best time for this type of fishing, it is a fact that the streamerette can be effective at other times as well. I well remember such an occasion. It was very early one morning, shortly after

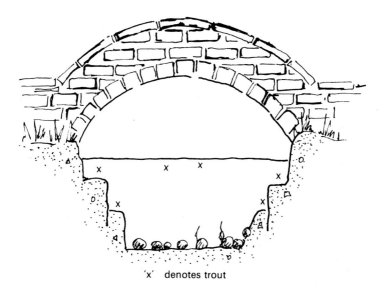

'x' denotes trout

Fig. 26 Under the bridge

Trout are inclined to lie along stone or concrete ledges at various depths and also close to the surface in the shadow cast by the bridge

97

dawn, and I was fishing Wiskoy Creek in the USA. It was mid-summer and the morning was beautiful and clear. My path down to the stream took me over an old wooden bridge made up of planks that had seen better days – there were wide gaps between them. I looked down between the gaps into a deep pool beneath the bridge. The sides of the pool were of shelving rock that disappeared into the depths. Several large trout were lying quite deep along the shelving rock, probably at least 6 ft (2 m) down.

I made my way upstream of the bridge and put up a large streamerette. I then used the same technique you have just been using: I paid out line and let the fly pass right under the bridge until it reached the other side. After a short pause to let the fly sink low in the water, I started an erratic retrieve.

You can imagine the shock I received when the water under the bridge suddenly seemed to explode. I am sure the spray must have reached the underside of the bridge. The fish I had hooked made a series of leaping jumps under the bridge, which were most difficult to control. After the most amazing fight I was able to net the fish out safely – a wild rainbow of over 2 lb (1 kg).

Perhaps, if you ever fish for rainbows in the local reservoir, you should try the streamerette – it would seem that it might be successful.

Before we recommence operations, let us move downstream a little to point F. The opposite bank from point C to B is well undercut and quite deep. We can make a series of casts to that bank between the two points, then retrieve the fly back across the stream. The current will keep the line taut so all you have to concentrate on is a good erratic retrieve.

No, that was not a very good effort. You allowed the current to take over the fly, and although you were working it well, the result was little different from using a wet fly. You must remember at all times that you are trying to simulate the movements of a small fish-fry: your retrieve must be faster and more erratic so as to overcome, and cut across, the current. Try it again.

That's a lot better. It doesn't matter if the fly is sometimes on the surface – just as long as it keeps darting about.

Well, that bank didn't produce anything for us, but it was a good place to try. Using these tactics we have to search every deep hole and undercut bank that we come across. There is no deep pool under the bridge, just white water over that pile of rocks; the deep pools are downstream the other side. Let's go back to the car for some hot coffee – afterwards we can fish below the bridge.

If you look below the bridge you will see that the stream really opens out. The rocks under the bridge have created a miniature waterfall. At point I it is quite shallow, but the centre current at point H to J has scoured out a deep channel. I have been here in the summer when the water was considerably lower and it was deep even then. The side eddy at point G is even deeper, and almost still water: a very interesting part of the stream.

I suggest that we cast from point I, across the current to point J, then retrieve back through the tail of the fast water.

current

Fig. 27 The waterfall

Trout will lie at the base of the falls, just downsteam of the cascading water. This type of lie is an ideal feeding station, as food is slowly released into the current from the turbulence

99

I don't think that we will pick up a fish in the fast water, but it would be wrong to ignore the water in front of us just because the eddy is more attractive. We can fish the eddy afterwards.

Those last two casts were very good. I liked the way the fly skipped through the fast water. It's hard to make the fly swim deep through the current: if you delay the retrieve the fly will swing down below us into shallow water.

That's a good cast too, right into the tail of the fast water. Bring the fly back quickly with a series of jerks. That's right, the fly is playing on the surface just – *another fish!*

Oh, what a shame, it's so small! Never mind, handle him very gently and slide him back in the water. That's amazing – you wouldn't believe that such a small fish would take so large a fly. If it had really been a fish-fry he could never have swallowed it. I wonder what they think when they take food that size. Perhaps they don't think at all, it's a matter of pure instinct.

Why are we using a streamerette instead of wet flies? I expected you to ask that question. It's not easy to answer in just a few words. I would like to relate an incident to you that will fully illustrate the reasoning behind our choice.

It was very early in the season, with the usual unsettled weather, when a friend and I had decided to fish a stream that flowed into a small lake in southern Ontario.

There was a small, wooden bridge supported on sunken, wood pylons that bridged the stream as it flowed into the small lake. Standing on the bridge I could see a number of good-size trout, at least six or seven, lying in a group among the sunken pylons. At first sight they appeared to be dormant, but small movements indicated that this was not so.

I called out to my companion on the bank and reported the position of the trout below me. While I looked down to watch the results he cast a wet fly between the pylons and retrieved it with a series of darting movements. The fly passed alongside the trout but brought no results. The fly was certainly seen by the trout – a couple of them even moved slightly away from it – but no attempt was made to take it or even to follow it. Several casts were made, but the result was the same each time.

I then called out and suggested that the wet fly be changed to a small lure, or streamerette. As soon as the lure was cast and retrieved through the pylons, several fish turned towards it. Before it had moved very far it was hit quite savagely by one of the larger fish.

This incident is hard to analyse to reach a firm conclusion, but I believe that early-season trout are not too interested in flies that simulate food that is not yet available to them. During the very early season there is a decided lack of underwater insect activity, and I do not believe the trout are expecting such food, or even looking for it. I also believe that their generally poor condition does not induce them to hunt small morsels of food until the supply is adequate and worth the energy expended.

The larger lure may be taken for two reasons. Obviously it represents a more substantial piece of food, and may be worth the effort needed to secure it, but I don't think that is the whole story. There is the very real probability that the trout resent any invasion of small-fry as a threat to their future food supply. In their early-season condition they do not wish to compete for food with eager, young fry. Consequently, they automatically attack any intruders they see.

So we use the streamerette to search out those deeper areas where the larger fish choose to lie pending their return to top condition. It is an invasion of their privacy – and we hope it will receive the full treatment in response!

Let's now try a cast to that eddy at point G, it looks a very good spot for a fish. It's very deep. If I were you I would cast slightly upstream into the rough water above point H, then let the current take the fly into the eddy. That's a good cast, just where we wanted it. Now we will wait for the fly to sink as deep as possible before it begins to leave the eddy. Let's give it plenty of time. I would like to think we could place the fly right on the bottom before we retrieve it to the surface.

Right, let's have that fly moving as fast as possible, and retrieve with short, sharp pulls – fast and erratic. I can now see it on the surface. Retrieve it right out of the eddy so that we can try the cast again. We can't always expect immediate results – I'm sure there are fish over there.

Yes, I would cast to the same place again, it takes the fly nicely into the eddy. We will give it a little longer to sink this time, perhaps we were not as deep as we thought. Right, let's start the retrieve. That's it, fast, short pulls right up to the – *that's it*! *He's on*!

Keep a tight line on him, he hasn't anywhere to go. Look at that rod bend! He's a good one, you must have taken him as the fly rose off the bottom. He's way down – deeper than I thought. He's coming up now. That's right, lead him below the fast water, he's finished now. I have the net – he's safely in, well done!

That's the best fish I have seen from this water, but see how lean he is? In three months time he will be well over $1\frac{1}{2}$ lb (0.7 kg). I say we put him back, let him have a few months to put on weight – and we will have the chance of him again. Good, he looked so pleased to get away!

Well, not a bad way to end the afternoon. It's been cold but most enjoyable. Let's go back to the car and warm up. Later this evening we can discuss the streamerette and other fish-fry simulators.

CHAPTER 10

THE STREAMERETTE

'Streamers' and 'bucktails' came originally from the USA and have proved time and time again that they are great takers of fish. They are now in use the world over, are very common in Australia and New Zealand, and are finding popularity on UK reservoirs. In New Zealand they have evolved to a new type of lure, the 'matuka', a very neat way to tie a streamer. However, there is a common factor to wherever these flies are fished: the fish are either free-taking rainbows, brook trout or other, rather naïve, chars. It is only occasionally that brown trout fall for this type of fly. Then it is usually the large, old cannibal or the reservoir-stocked fish. For some reason the brown trout in reservoirs take on some of the characteristics of their fellow rainbows.

The standard bucktail or streamer has never had a great deal of success with UK river trout. In fact, it has not been too successful in the USA, as far as brown trout are concerned, except on such large and wild rivers as the Ausable. These very large wilderness rivers are an exception.

Some years ago an American, Sam Slaymaker III, decided to design a bucktail that would simulate a baby brown trout. His reasoning was that brown trout are notorious for eating their off-spring and a lure was the best way to simulate them. An amazing amount of study went

'Little brown trout' streamerette

into this enterprise, and the result was a highly-acclaimed bucktail tied on a very small hook. It was very small for an American bucktail, which are usually anything from $1\frac{1}{2}$ to 4 in (38 to 102 mm) long. There is no doubt that the Slaymaker bucktail, tied on a size-12 hook, made a breakthrough as far as brown trout are concerned.

I used the Slaymaker 'little brown trout' for many years with very good results. The change to the streamerette came about after I became acquainted with a series of flies called the 'Thunder Creek series'. These flies allowed a bait-fish imitation to be tied even smaller, and much more sparsely. The Thunder Creek flies were not so much a series of flies as a rather novel way of dressing them. The streamerette is basically Sam Slaymaker's ideas combined with the Thunder Creek form of dressing (see Fig. 28).

The dressing for the streamerette is as follows:

Tying-silk : Red.
Hook : 12 or 14 long shank.

104

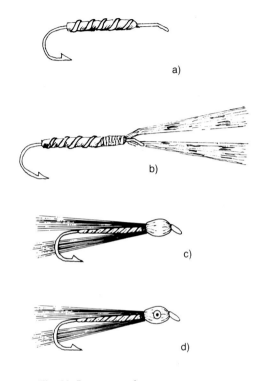

Fig. 28 Brown-trout-fry streamerette

Body   :   Flat gold tinsel, ribbed with oval gold tinsel,
                 well lacquered.
Upper wing: Coloured impala tail – a few strands of yel-
                 low, over which are a few strands of red,
                 topped by a few strands of black.
Lower wing: A few strands of white impala tail.
Eye   :   Celullose – large yellow, with black dot in
                 centre.

The following tips on construction may be helpful (see Fig.
28): (a) shows the body built from the bend to two-thirds
along the hook shank; (b) shows the impala hair bound to

105

the front one-third of the hook shank and pointing forward (*important note*: the upper half of the impala hair is tied down with the colours in *reverse order*, so that when the hair is brought back over the shank it will be in the correct sequence); (c) shows that when the hair is brought back over the shank it should be pulled back firmly to form a neat head – keep the white below and the colours above. Tie down at the neck by bringing the red tying-silk through the hair. Finish off the neck with a whip finish. Finally, give the head several coats of clear lacquer, allowing it to dry well between coats.

With coloured, cellulose varnish, paint a large eye on both sides of the head as shown in (d).

It should be especially noted that to be most effective this fly needs to be dressed very sparsely. The aim should be to create a gold body only thinly veiled with impala hair. The eye should be very prominent.

When in action in the water, this fly gives a wraith type of illusion: a gold body with touches of red and yellow, and an upper part of black over a white belly, the main feature being a large eye. We hope that is how the trout expects to see a brown-trout fry.

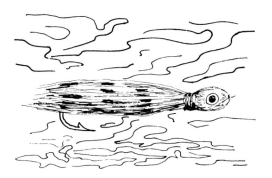

Fig. 29 The underwater profile of the streamerette

The following incident will show how effective these tiny bait-fish simulators can be. Once, while fishing a mountain stream, my way was blocked by a fall of large boulders in the stream itself. I couldn't pass along the bank because of the dense vegetation, nor could I cross the stream due to the depth and the current. I decided to clamber over the boulders rather than go back. At the time I had been using a small fish-fry simulator and it was still tied to the end of my leader, so rather than hook such a fly into the cork handle of my rod, I paid out several yards of line and let it trail downstream. I was halfway over the boulders on all fours, with the rod under my arm, when I felt insistent tugging at the rod tip. Yes, a trout had taken that fish-fry as it played on the surface below me! Can you imagine playing a trout while trying to crawl over a large boulder?

Although there is usually a lack of other types of fry in a small, trout stream, this is not always the case. The common minnow may also be present; so might the fry of other coarse fish. One stream I have fished in Herefordshire has a very large population of chub. The Thunder Creek style of tying is ideal to simulate these other varieties. All that needs to be done is to vary the body tinsel from gold to silver, then to vary the colour of the impala hair. For coarse fish, two colours are usually sufficient: black over white. All these small-fry have a very large eye, out of all proportion to their size.

These flies do take a little longer to tie, but they are well worth the trouble. They are almost indestructible and will last many seasons. If you don't tie your own flies and are in the habit of giving your instructions to a professional tyer, expect to pay a little more for these flies – a professional's time is money.

I hope these tiny fry-simulators will bring you the sport I have experienced with them.

107

HOOKING, PLAYING
AND LANDING

Hooking

Before we can consider hooking a fish, it is necessary to take a look at the hook itself. Today there are a large number of manufacturers producing a bewildering array of hooks in a multitude of designs. Some of the latest 'advances' in hook manufacture have little bearing on the angler's needs, and what are presented as scientific break-throughs are, in fact, little more than new manufacturing techniques. The angler's needs are basically simple: a fisherman needs a strong hook correctly formed, of good temper and size, of correct weight, with a barb of the right shape and sharpness.

Let us review these features one at a time. A good hook needs to be formed with a forged bend even when the lightest hook wire is used in manufacture, as this is the weakest part of the hook and the most vulnerable to breakage. The temper of the hook wire should be such that when the hook is placed in the tying vice and the shank flicked with the finger nail a decided 'spring' is detected. The hook must be available in a weight that suits its intended use; lightweight for dry flies, heavier wire for wet flies and lures. The barb, the most important part of the hook, must be small and distinctly formed with a sharp point.

The barb needs more consideration than it normally

receives. Under ideal conditions a barb is totally unnecessary, in fact it hinders hooking by needing extra pressure to penetrate beyond the barb. As ideal conditions require a constant tight line with never a fraction of slack – a condition that rarely exists – a barb is used to make the hook more secure in the fish. It therefore follows that the smaller a barb can be made, consistent with holding power, the better.

Hooks direct from the manufacturer are seldom as sharp as they can be made by the angler. All hooks benefit from a light touch of a sharpening stone, and a good time to do this is before the hook is placed in the tying vice. Once the fly is in the flybox it will need constant inspection and the odd touch with the sharpening stone, which is especially true in the case of wet flies where slight rust may occur. When sharpening a hook be sure to sharpen the inside of the barb only, and stroke the stone towards the point. This will cause the point itself slightly to point outwards and increase its hooking power.

The length of the hook shank has a direct bearing on the penetrating power of the point, the longer the shank the greater the pressure exerted on the point. In most cases the length of the shank is dictated by the fly to be tied on the hook, but whenever possible 2 × long shanks (twice standard length), should be used. Wet flies present no difficulty in this respect, but many dry flies are out of proportion if tied with such elongated bodies. One way to overcome this problem is to tie the fly on the back three quarters up the hook shank, leaving a small portion of the shank protruding beyond the finished head. The effectiveness of the fly is in no way impaired; in fact its balance is somewhat improved.

Hooks are available with a variety of bend shapes, but for flyfishing small streams we only need to concern ourselves with two of these, the round bend and the sneck bend. Without doubt the sneck bend has superior hooking power.

The disadvantages, however, of using the sneck bend are numerous: quite apart from the fly tying difficulties, the balance of a small fly is badly disturbed by the poor weight distribution. Wet flies on this hook tend to swim on their sides with rather a peculiar motion, and dry flies often fail to 'cock' beautifully on the surface. The river angler cannot go far wrong if all flies are tied on round bend hooks.

The size of hook is determined by the size of the fly to be tied on it. It is a complete fallacy that larger hooks will more securely hold the fish – the average stream trout is securely held on any hook between size 20 and size 10. If the fly is required to be small the hook size must correspond to it, hooking power does not enter the equation.

It is appreciated that not all anglers tie their own flies, but the foregoing should still be the criteria demanded of shop-bought flies. Because a fly comes from a professional tyer is unfortunately no guarantee that it will meet the requirements of a discerning angler; the hook on which the fly is tied is a very cheap part of our tackle – but probably the most important part!

Playing

Before we consider the playing of a fish, we should clearly establish in our minds what we are attempting to accomplish. A fish is 'played' to enable us to take it from the water, but we cannot do this immediately it is hooked for two reasons. Firstly, although the fish is almost weightless in the water, its struggles plus the weight of the water itself are often enough to break the fine tippet at the end of our cast. Secondly, the same struggles and water weight tend to tear the hook from the hold it has taken. By playing the fish we are able to subdue its struggles to the point where it can be drawn over the net, or to the hand, without the risk of breakage or of the hook tearing out.

The above may sound elementary, but it is surprising how many trout fishermen take the words 'playing a fish' literally, and derive pleasure from letting the fish run wherever it wants while they play with it. Not only is this extremely bad sportsmanship, but it gives no thought to the wellbeing of the trout which, after all, is a living creature. Perhaps we might be better off if we used the words subduing the fish, instead of playing.

A trout should always be removed from the water as quickly as possible, consistent with avoiding breakage and/or tearing out the hook. To accomplish this we must, by necessity, be prepared to let the trout have line, but we should contest every inch of line we give. With smaller trout it is always best to 'handline' rather than play the fish from the reel: larger and heavier fish are best controlled direct from the reel. The ratchet of a reel seems to cause erratic behaviour by the fish, perhaps the vibrations are carried down the line – the ideal reel is ratchet free when giving line, drag being maintained by a slipping clutch. This point should be borne in mind when buying yourself a new reel. Such reels are readily available and any good tackle dealer can advise you on this. An alternative is to take the ratchet off and apply drag with the fingertips on the rim of the reel.

To handline a trout, the line should pass between the forefinger and thumb of the hand holding the rod, and be drawn in or released by the other hand. If a light pressure is maintained between the forefinger and thumb, any slackness in the line will be kept to a minimum. This is obviously a very sensitive way to play a trout as every movement of the fish is clearly felt between the fingers. The recovered line is just dropped at the feet until an opportune moment when it can be reeled in. When fishing the dry fly upstream the dropped line presents no problem as it is carried downstream of the angler; when fishing a wet fly or lure downstream it is best to reel in slack from time to time.

111

The metabolism of a fish is geared for short bursts of quick activity, and prolonged expenditure of energy leads to complete exhaustion. If light pressure is maintained against the trout and breathing restricted by the hook pulling the mouth open, the fish will tire quickly. Also, the intense burst of energy expended to escape the sudden restriction often upsets the swim-bladder, which will leave the fish unstable in the water. When a trout is almost played out it will roll towards the surface on its side, if the head is then held above the water level a further lack of underwater oxygen takes its toll.

It must be appreciated that fish handled this roughly will rarely recover if returned to the water; the damage done is almost always fatal. If it is not intended to kill and eat the fish, or the fish is under-sized, it should never be played out to this level. Small fish can be drawn in quickly without fear of breakage, larger fish should be netted as quickly as possible if they are to be released.

When playing a fish only a light tension need be applied to the line, the struggles of the fish against the spring of the rod tip exert the main pressure. This built-in spring, and the elasticity of the nylon cast, act as a shock absorber against breakage. A rod held at a low angle, say 30 degrees, exerts much more pressure than a rod held at a higher angle. Many fishermen think that by holding the rod high throughout the fight they are consistently applying maximum pressure; not so, the angle should be varied as needed. It is often necessary to turn a fish that is running towards a bad snag. Use the rod to do this by lowering it to water level and applying side strain to the fish. If the fish is large and cannot be safely turned in this manner, then sometimes the giving of a yard of slack line will do the job. It may be that the fish, feeling no restriction, thinks the danger is past.

A trout that has run into underwater vegetation is always a problem. It is almost impossible to dislodge such a fish by applying direct pressure, the cast is probably wound round and round tough stems of the vegetation.

There are some standard remedies that can be tried. Slack line can be given in the hope the trout will swim out of his own accord. You can try tapping the rod butt while holding a tight line. The vibrations might make the fish move out but are more likely to make it swim deeper into the vegetation. Some anglers throw stones at the fish, but this is seldom effective. If the water can be waded, the best thing is to approach the weeds, reeling in the line, and try to release the trout by pulling the vegetation up. As stated above, this is a real problem, and only luck will determine whether or not your cast remains unbroken.

Landing

After we have played out we have to land the fish, but before we discuss this in any detail let us take a look at the landing net we will probably use. The river fisherman needs to carry a folding net that can be slung from his belt, bag or creel, and the type that opens out to a triangle is by far the best. If it has an extending handle, so much the better.

The only other practical folding net has a solid hoop to hold the netting and, although this type of net folds for carrying, the round hoop remains rigid. No matter how this type of net is carried the hoop is an infernal nuisance to the wading fisherman, and it is not recommended.

The net comes into use at a critical juncture of our activities – should it fail the result will be a lost fish. For this reason we must look upon the net as a vital part of our tackle and look after it accordingly, or it will malfunction just when we need it most. The mesh net should be examined frequently, its strength tested and any small tears repaired. It is a good idea to tie a pierced lead or lead substitute bullet to the base of the mesh, as this will sink the mesh quickly in

113

the water. The point where the side arms are hinged requires a little reel oil from time to time so that they will swing out easily with a flick of the wrist. When a net has an extending handle it is most important that this is lightly greased so that it slides freely. With attention paid to these points the net will function smoothly, and can be brought into action using only one hand.

The easiest way to net a fish is to unsling the net just before it is required, while the fish is still a few yards or metres away. Sink the net in front of you so that it rests on the river bed, with the handle upwards against your body, or gripped between your knees. The played out fish is then drawn towards you, head raised above water level until it is over the submerged net. A smooth raising of the net will complete the operation.

A very useful tip is to trap the line with your forefinger against the cork grip of the rod as you draw the fish over the net, having first made sure that an armslength or so of line has been stripped off the reel and allowed to hang down. As soon as the fish is safely in the net release the trapped line. In this manner all tension is taken off the rod tip and the risk of breakage is kept to a minimum.

Should you fail to net the fish at the first attempt, don't panic. Let the fish have a little line then repeat the procedure taking care to make your movements smooth and deliberate.

If the above-described netting has been correctly carried out, you will be left in the awkward position of a rod in one hand and a netted fish in the other, both connected by the line. When you are prepared to wade ashore this will present no difficulty but if, as is so often the case, you do not wish to disturb the water, it is a different matter. To overcome this problem, place the rod into the loops provided on most fishing vests, hold the net handle firmly under the left arm, then using both hands deal with the fish.

Whenever it is your intention to kill a trout then do so

before you attempt to remove the hook. In the case of a small trout the easiest way to kill it is to insert the forefinger into the mouth placing the thumb on the back of the head, a hard backward bend of the head will kill the fish instantly. A larger fish will need a sharp tap on the base of the skull with a priest. Always kill a fish while holding it in the meshes of the net otherwise you might lose it. The practice of banging the head against the nearest stone is to be deplored, it is not only ineffective, it is downright cruel.

When handling fish that are to be returned to the water always make sure that your hands are wet and never squeeze the fish. If you hear a squeaking sound from the fish it means internal organs have been ruptured, kill the fish instantly. Never, never, return a live fish by throwing it into the water, place it gently into the water with the head held facing upstream, and support it in that position until it swims away of its own accord.

Always treat a trout with respect, it was a worthy adversary and deserves your full consideration.

APPENDIX B

WADING

There are two types of wading: good, thoughtful wading is an aid to catching fish; bad wading can thoroughly spoil a day's sport. There are, unfortunately, too many anglers who can't resist entering the water immediately – it's the first thing they do when they reach the water's edge. In fact, it should be the last thing done after a full appraisal of the stream and the careful, advance planning of tactics.

The object should be to wade as little as possible, only using the ability to wade in order to reach the most advantageous casting positions. It must be appreciated that wading disturbs fish no matter how carefully it is done. It is impossible to make movements under water without those tremors being sensed by wary trout.

It is always good practice to cast first to those areas where one intends to wade later. It is common on small streams to find areas of water near the bank that are very shallow, usually over large stones that have been swept downstream during spates. Very often, standing in a few inches of water, one can cast over an area where later it is intended to wade – sometimes with surprising results. At least any fish present will have been tried for, a much better idea than having them scoot away to avoid being trodden on!

An angler who thoughtlessly enters the stream, who

The author fishes the dry fly. The point where a tributary
enters the main stream is always a good spot to
try for territorial trout

clumsily splashes and moves stones underfoot, will be casting
to water empty of fish. Any fish in the area will dart away
upstream well outside of casting range. Worse, as the angler
finds no sport and moves further along the stream, the fish
will continue to move ahead away from the angler's range of
activities. A great deal can be done to remedy this situation.
Although good wading is almost a science, any angler who
obeys a few basic rules and employs a little thought can enjoy
a good day's sport.

Obviously there are a number of 'don'ts'. Don't wade
unless you have to. If you want to progress further upstream,
or downstream, then leave the water and walk along the
bank. Even if you have no intention of fishing a particular
stretch of water don't wade through it: you will disturb the
fish for a surprising distance ahead. When you walk along

the bank remember that waders are clumsy things and that your footfalls are probably much heavier than you think. It's always a good idea to walk along as far from the edge of the bank as possible.

Don't wade deeper than necessary, and keep away from fast water as much as possible. The depth of the water may not be dangerous, but the pressure against your waders makes it very difficult to place your feet carefully. It should also be remembered that the stream bed is uneven. If you are almost to your maximum depth one further step may well be over the top of your waders – and that can be very uncomfortable! Fast water, even shallow, fast water, exerts much more pressure than you think. It will cause a stumble that results in splashing as you recover your balance.

I well remember fishing a very wide, shallow stream in the Catskill Mountains. The average depth was no more than a couple of feet. Together with my companion, I had waded out further and further from the bank as we 'swept' our wet flies downstream. The current was very fast indeed, and it was becoming difficult to keep our balance even in such shallow water. We therefore decided to move back towards the bank. It proved impossible to wade across the current and at the same time keep our footing; at one stage my partner was on hands and knees in 2 ft (0.6 m) of water! We were forced to wade diagonally across, and downstream, in order to reach the bank. This manoeuvre took us many yards downstream and we were lucky that the depth was even and that there were no holes. Yes, even shallow, fast water can be very deceptive.

Another 'don't' for your consideration: don't shuffle your feet along the stream bed. This may seem a safe way to wade but it is not as safe as picking your feet up and carefully testing where you put them down. No foot should be put down finally until you are absolutely sure it will be on sound footing. Quite large stones have little weight in water and move very easily. Picking your feet up slowly and gently, and placing them down in the same way, causes very little disturbance and will enable you to approach the fish more closely.

As you wade, always look down to see where you are going. It sounds a stupid remark, but it is surprising how many anglers move forward automatically as they fish, particularly when fishing the wet fly. Always fish out your cast carefully before moving, then forget the fishing for a moment until you have carefully moved to your new position. Then it is time to cast again. A pair of polaroid glasses will help you see the stream bed more easily – in fact, as a safety precaution some sort of glasses should always be worn when casting a fly.

I once had the pleasure of fishing a wilderness river on Victoria Island, British Columbia, about 5 miles (8 km) into dense bush country. My host assured me that the river was very rarely fished and that the trout should be very obliging. When we reached the water's edge I was immediately impressed with the scene in front of me: a beautiful stretch of water with a large rock protruding from the centre. I decided to stay and fish that very spot. I had no need to wade except in the water's edge. My host wished me luck, said he would see me later, then waded into the water and splashed his way upstream. I watched him disappear round the bend and had to wait quietly for the disturbance to die down.

I spent the whole morning in that delightful spot. The scenery was fantastic and there were no sounds except for the gurgling water and the birds. By the time my host returned I had taken fourteen trout from around that centre rock. The fishing was easy and the trout took an artificial fly with ready abandon. My host had not raised a single fish! I decided to make no comment, but it taught me that even wilderness fish will not take kindly to heavy, splashy wading – British educated trout even less so.

I have always considered a wading staff to be essential to good wading, even in a shallow small stream. Without doubt they are a necessary aid to the anglers who fish large, strong rivers of great depth. But that is not the only use for a staff. The right kind of staff can probe depths, steady your balance as you move, and prevent that stumbling splash when the current catches you unawares.

The problem lies in finding the right kind of staff. The beautifully-made, and expensive, wading staffs that are usually offered for sale seem to be designed especially for those deep, strong rivers. The manufacturers do not appear to take any other form of wading into account. Long ago I decided that the ideal wading staff for a small stream needed to be of a different design, but I was unable to find a manufactured staff that satisfied me.

I wanted to have a staff light enough to be slung from an elastic lanyard across my shoulders – a lanyard that would extend as I used the staff. When not in use, I wanted the staff to be of a design that enabled it to be dropped to float behind me in the water. It was required to have a rubber tip so that no disturbance was made when probing depths. Some sort of depth indicator was also required.

I settled the problem with a couple of evenings' work (see Fig. 30). As an added bonus the cost was negligible.

A $\frac{1}{2}$-in (13-mm) diameter garden cane was cut to a 56-in (1.4-m) length and well sanded down. A rubber walking-stick ferrule was then well glued to one end. The opposite

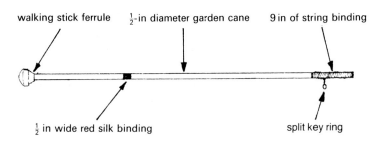

Fig. 30 The home-made wading staff

120

end was neatly bound, in touching turns, with rough string to make a 9-in (230-mm) handle. The whip finish to the string incorporated a split key-ring to take the lanyard. I then measured my waders from the sole to a distance of 3 in (76 mm) from the top. This measurement was transferred to the staff and marked by a $\frac{1}{2}$-in (13-mm) binding of red silk.

Finally, the staff was given three coats of good varnish, including the string handle. The lanyard was made from a length of round elastic cord. Three lengths of 1 yd (1 m) were cut and knotted together at one end. A plait was then made and secured with a knot at the other end. Once the elastic plait was passed through the split ring it was easy to adjust the length I wanted across my shoulders and to tie off accordingly.

In use I find that this staff can be extended on its lanyard to probe the water ahead. The red indicator tells me if the water will be over my waders. While I am casting it is dropped to my side and it floats in the water behind me. Last, but not least, it does not clatter against rocks and stones – ideal!

It was mentioned in the chapter, 'Tackle', that the ideal wader sole was made of thick felt. We used to be able to obtain this felt from piano manufacturers and repairers: it was very hard, white felt about $\frac{1}{2}$ in (13 mm) in thickness. The procedure was to cut two pieces from a 12-in (0.3-m) square. Each wader sole and the felt were then treated with impact adhesive – the felt required about three applications. After the wader soles and the felt were brought together it was a simple task to cut round the outline of the sole with a sharp knife and throw the surplus felt away.

There is nothing that excels felt for non-slip wading on rocks and stones, and it is really surprising how hard wearing the stuff is. I have found that the felt sole will often last longer than the waders themselves. As was said previously, the difficulty lies in obtaining the correct felt.

APPENDIX C

CASTING

It is not the intention in these pages to give basic casting instruction. It is assumed that the reader is already a flyfisher with some experience, either on rivers or still water. If this is not so, then no casting instruction given here could be of benefit to a rank beginner. Practical instruction from an experienced instructor would be called for. Casting can certainly be improved by the written word, but the 'feel' of the basic action must come from practical sessions under the eye of a teacher.

The aim of this appendix is to iron out some of the difficulties, real or imagined, that arise when a lighter and shorter rod are used for the first time. I sincerely hope the reader will give these light-weight rods a try – they make so much difference to the sport and pleasure of fishing a small stream. A 10-in (255-mm) wild brownie will put up the fight of a lifetime when caught on a 7-ft (2-m) rod, a no. 5 line, and a 5× tippet – in every way equal to a 2-lb (0.9-kg) fish caught on a heavier 9–10-ft (2.7–3-m) rod, a no. 8 line, with a 2× tippet to match.

Most problems encountered with a small rod stem from the anglers themselves. They know that the rod is different so they subconsciously alter their whole casting action. Then, when things start to go wrong, they make further adjustments. It doesn't take too long for the rod to be classed as a toy and useless. Nothing could be further from the truth – these rods are not toys!

It was mentioned in the chapter, 'Tackle', that my own choice of rod is a 5-ft (1.5-m) split cane weighing $1\frac{5}{8}$ oz (46 g). This little one-piece rod works in perfect harmony with a Hardy featherweight reel loaded with 20 yd (18.3 m) of no. 5 line plus backing. A toy? Not under any circumstances! I am now so attached to it that I rarely use anything else the whole season through. It handles all my trout with ease – and I catch my fair share of the bigger fellows. I'm confident that no trout I encounter will get the better of me due to the rod I use. If my rod is a serious working tool, why should a 7-ft (2-m) rod be classed as a toy? Is it because they make casting difficult? No, not at all – it's all in the mind!

The most common error seen when anglers use a short rod for the first time is a violent action of the whole casting arm. The subconscious mind tells them they must really put some muscle to work – the rod can't do it, so they must do it for the rod. At the same time they have a mental picture of the line being too close to their head, so the rod must be raised higher to keep the line up. The result is usually a casting action that swings the rod from the shoulder – forward then backward in a horizontal plane – while the hand gripping the rod is held at ear level. It looks something like an early western pioneer driving a team of mules with a whip!

None of this is necessary. The length of arc at the rod tip of a 10-ft (3-m) rod, during normal casting, certainly exceeds the length of arc made by a 7-ft (2-m) rod used the same way. It therefore appears that the tip of the 10-ft (3-m) rod moves faster, but this does not mean that more force is needed to obtain the same result from a 7-ft (2-m) rod. The actions of the two rods are different (see Fig. 31).

Many years ago when split cane was cheap, all manner of rods found their way onto the market. Some were good, but

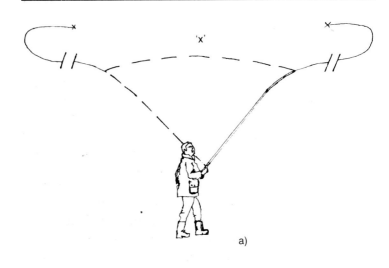

a)

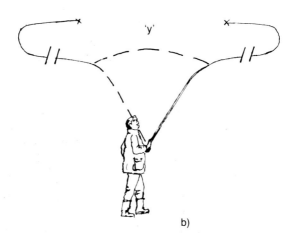

b)

Fig. 31 The casting arc
(a) The 10-ft (3-m) rod
Note the greater bend in the rod compared to illustration (b) and also the resulting wider loop than shown in illustration (b)
(b) The 7-ft (2-m) rod
Note that the arc 'Y' is less than the arc 'X' shown in illustration (a)

many others had 'actions' totally unsuited to their length. Today, we are not in that position – split cane is terribly expensive and is invariably used for best rods only; glass fibre and carbon are more easily controlled in manufacture. The 'action' of the rod you buy today is almost sure to be correct for the length of rod and the type of fishing for which it was intended. 'Actions' do vary, and intentionally so, but the difference is related to the weight of line specified, the length of cast envisaged, and the type of presentation required. Almost all modern rods will cast their specified lines without any undue force being required from the angler.

The 7-ft (2-m) rod will normally have a much faster action than the longer rod. For our purposes one can think of this action as being 'stiffer', although this is not actually correct – it is a great deal more subtle than that. In use, the upper part of the small rod will not bend to the same extent as the upper section of the longer rod. In consequence, although the longer rod tip moves through a larger arc, the force it exerts on the line is applied more gradually. The faster action of the shorter rod exerts the necessary force much more quickly (see Fig. 31).

What does this mean to us? Well, first of all excessive force when casting is completely unnecessary – the design of the rod will take care of its shorter length. Because the rod is 'fast' the line acceleration is also fast, and slightly less time is needed between the forward- and backward-cast. Waving the rod from the shoulder completely destroys this 'fast action' – hence the problems. Due to the fast line-acceleration during normal casting, the line will travel in a tight loop between 5 and 7 ft (1.5 m and 2 m) above the angler's head. There is certainly no necessity to raise the rod into the air to gain height (see Fig. 31).

A well-known American tackle company used to hold casting seminars on a local river. This company was famous for its short-to-medium-length split-cane rods, and each new owner was invited to join a seminar. During instruction the pupils were encouraged to stand in the water, facing downstream, to get the feel of the line on water. One of the staff instructors used to ask the pupils to imagine they were standing with their backs against a 10-ft (3-m) solid wall, and to make sure that their back-casts were thrown back high enough to clear the wall. He was also insistent that they kept their upper arms fairly close to their sides. Any offending pupils were warned that if they persisted in lifting their upper arms they would be required to put a ten-dollar bill under their arm while they cast. The current in the river was quite fast – enough said! I can offer no better advice – that instructor knew how to teach.

A common misconception that often gives rise to problems with a shorter rod, is that the heavier a line is the further it will cast. Although the line is, in fact, the 'weight' the rod casts, it is not necessarily true that the heavier line will cast further – it completely depends on the rod. It is somewhat confusing to find that the line recommendation for a 7-ft (2-m) rod is, perhaps, a no. 4 *or* a no. 5 *or* a no. 6. The temptation may be to use the no. 6 line in the belief it will cast more easily, and cast further.

The truth of the matter is a little more complex. Such a rod would be designed to carry a no. 6 line, but only 30 ft (9.1 m) of such line outside the rod tip satisfies that rating. As a rule of thumb you can say that every 6 ft (1.8 m) of line out equals one unit of rating, so false-casting 36 ft (12 yd, 11 m) of the no. 6 line with the same rod would be the approximate equivalent of using a no. 7 line – too heavy for the rod in question. Of course, this only applies to normal casting or false-casting – shooting extra line is another matter.

A heavy line, one that is too heavy for the rod, will tend to drop on both the forward- and the backward-cast, decreasing distance rather than increasing it. If you are in the habit of false-casting 36 ft (11 m), and your rod is rated as above, then a no. 5 line will give much better results. Use 42 ft (14 yd, 12.8 m) during your false-casts and you will need to reduce to a no. 4 line. So the rating of no. 4, no. 5 or no. 6 is completely accurate – it depends a great deal on your length of cast. Also remember that these rod ratings are intended to apply to the 'average' angler. There is probably no such person. A 6-ft (1.8-m) angler with bulging muscles may well be quite a delicate caster, whereas his friend, who is a weedy individual, casts like a demon.

I can only offer myself as an example. Over the years my casting has become more delicate as my movements have become more precise. I now try to make the rod do practically all the work. My own little rod is rated for a no. 6 line, but I invariably use a no. 5 to obtain the best results, and this is not because I am in the habit of false-casting a long line. My own interpretation of these facts is that if the full power

The author and an uninvited friend fishing on Oaka Creek, New York State, USA

127

of the rod is allowed to develop, then the weight cast (the line) does not have to be so great. Line acceleration makes up the difference.

So, do not be absolutely committed to using the line weight recommended for your rod. Borrow a couple of lines, or buy a couple of cheap ones to experiment with. One rating either up or down could make a considerable difference to your casting.

Many anglers decide on a line that is heavier than they need in the belief that it helps their casting into, or across, a strong wind. This is just not so – let's think about it. A line not only has weight but it also has mass, which results in wind resistance. A line that is a no. 6 has a larger diameter, and consequently more mass, than a no. 5. For our purposes let us think of this mass as 'bulk'. It then becomes readily apparent that a 'bulky' object offers more wind resistance, and is more easily affected by the wind, than a less 'bulky' object. While it might be true that a heavier line is projected with more force, that force does not compensate for the resistance set up by its mass. In practice you will find that the correct line for your rod, and for your casting action, will handle better in a wind than putting up a heavier line.

If wind is ever a real bother to you, then try the old remedy of side-casting close to the surface of the water. In a cross-wind from the right I invariably side-cast and keep the line very low – it does away with the constant concern for my right ear!

You may have made a mental note of the comment, in the chapter, 'Tackle', about taking 6 to 8 in (152 to 203 mm) off the end of your flyline. In years gone by when silk lines were in regular use, this was a necessity due to their irregular lengths. The plastic flylines of today are so controlled in manufacture that normally no adjustment is necessary. However, a flyline designed for use with a standard solid-nylon leader behaves in a slightly different manner when used with a braided, tapered one. Perhaps the difference is caused by the thicker butt, or perhaps it is due to a difference in weight – I am not sure. At first I believed the cause was the braided leader being more supple; that may still be true. In use I found that the combination of line taper, followed by a level portion of line, followed once again by a pronounced taper, had an effect on the turnover of the line.

When the line was being false-cast in a tight loop the turnover within the loop was not as smooth and even as I would have wished. This in turn affected the presentation of the fly. I took a chance and reduced the level section of the line by a few inches. The result was readily apparent: I found that only a 6–8-in (152–203-mm) adjustment was necessary.

If you try this for yourself, don't dash in by immediately chopping that amount from your line. Be prudent, try a couple of inches first to see if you notice any improvement. Take off more than 8 in (203 mm) and you will create other problems, so be careful.

There is one problem that is very real with a short rod, the problem of line twist. For some reason it is the normal reaction for someone casting with a short rod to bring the rod forward, during the forward-cast, in a different plane than that used for the back-cast. The result is a slow circular movement of the rod tip. This action does not seem to occur when the same angler uses a longer rod.

The circular movement twists the line. The line in the air, due to its acceleration and turnover, does not twist. The twist is first noticed in the slack line between the reel and the first rod-ring. In severe cases this can be a real bird's nest. The cure lies in a correct casting action. If you find, during a day's fishing, that you have set up such a twist, it can be cleared by letting all the line that is already off your reel float away downstream – the water flow will straighten it out. The final cure lies in correcting your casting.

The difference a quality line can make to your casting

should never be under-estimated. There is an old saying, 'you get what you pay for' – how very true about flylines. The smooth, even, and supple nature of a first-quality line really enhances your casting and line handling. The turnover will be better, it will shoot line more easily, it will roll-cast more evenly, and it will land on the water more gently. Yes, 'you get what you pay for'. Don't economise on flylines, buy the best you can afford. Keep it clean by washing it from time to time in soapy water – a good, clean line will last many seasons.

A final tip on casting with a short rod. Because of the rod's lighter weight the angler may begin to let the rod drift too far back in the back-cast. At first this is not noticed, then the forward-cast starts to deteriorate. Because the rod is light-weight, and the cork grip is small, this is quite easy to correct – instead of placing your thumb along the top of the cork grip, use your forefinger. The forefinger is not able to bend back as far as your thumb can. For most people this is a very uncomfortable grip. Never mind, use it for a short period until you have regained the correct casting action.

Before I end these comments on casting, I would like to tell you of an incident that I have always remembered. When I was a very young man I stood by the water's side and watched a very elderly gentleman casting. His casting could only be described as exquisite, it was poetry in motion.

'How I wish I could cast as well as you do!' I called out to him.

He called back, 'practise hard for another forty years and you might be able to!'

130

WEATHER AND CONDITIONS

Not being, in any way whatever, an expert on the weather, I hesitated before writing this section. However, knowing how much my fishing has been influenced by the weather, in terms of fish caught, I felt that it would be very remiss on my part if I did not try to pass on the observations I have made over the years.

Heat and cold have an effect on trout, but only at times of extreme heat and cold is it really noticeable. I have taken good fish when the weather has been much too cold to fish in comfort. This applies particularly to rainbow trout and brook trout. I have taken good bags of these fish when there has been snow on the banks and slush floating in the stream. The brown trout is very sluggish at these temperatures, but will still feed to a certain extent. A very high temperature is a different matter: trout become dormant very quickly as the temperature of the water rises.

At Rainbow Ranch in Ontario I remember one very hot summer when at times the temperature was steady in the low nineties for days on end. One day I was amazed to see that all the fish in one of the lakes had gathered at the point where it was fed by a good-size stream. They had not entered the stream itself, but were lying just in the lake in less than 12 in (0.3 m) of water. There were so many fish in that one area that they were forced to lie side by side – it was one immense carpet of trout. They were so dormant that we had no difficulty in walking right up to them. Obviously the extreme heat was causing acute oxygen starvation. Fishing in such conditions would be a complete waste of time.

On the other hand, I have caught fish at Rainbow Ranch when it was so cold that the difficulty was thawing the ice from the rod rings between casts.

I am now convinced that a sustained high temperature will destroy the fishing much more quickly than a severe cold spell. Of course, it all depends on the normal conditions: what is a high or low temperature to a fish in Alaska is totally different from that experienced by a fish in the UK. The normal conditions must be taken into account when calculating what effect a very hot, or cold, temperature will have.

It must also be recognised that water temperature in a stream, unlike still water, is not influenced by hot or cold days to that extent. Very often, even a few consecutive days of extreme temperature will not influence the stream temperature to any marked degree – the main problem, as far as fishing on a very hot day is concerned, may well be the very bright sun. Trout do not like this brightness and will seek shelter from it.

Wind has a decided influence on our sport, but I have always noted that this is very closely tied in with the atmospheric pressure. I was once told that the prevailing wind over the UK was south-westerly. It might well be – but it has never seemed that way to me! As a small boy, fishing for roach with maggots, I was taught the following jingle:

> When the wind is North or East,
>   The fish bite the least.
> When the wind is from the South,
>   It blows the bait into the fish's mouth.

132

> When the wind is from the West,
> The fishing is the best!

An old-wife's tale? Possibly not. Trout do not like an approaching low-pressure system – they feed more consistently when the approaching system is of high pressure. In the UK most low-pressure systems seem to come from the North and East, so South or West winds may well offer an advantage.

You will have noticed that I have used the word 'approaching' several times. I believe that the 'approaching' system is far more important than the system that is already with us. When we are enjoying a current high-pressure weather system, trout will very often go off the feed apparently for no good reason. It often transpires that the good weather is coming to an end and a low-pressure system is forecast. Trout are very sensitive to such a change, several hours before the change actually takes place. For consistent feeding the pressure system has to be settled for at least twenty-four hours.

We have previously mentioned a very bright sun. I am sure that trout are very sensitive to such brightness for a number of reasons. Their constant awareness of danger must be foremost. Looking into a bright sky their vision is impaired and consequently approaching danger may not be seen in time. I have also formed the opinion that their eyes are extremely sensitive to light. Any living creature that can see well in the dark – and a trout most certainly can – does not enjoy bright conditions. So when you are fishing on one of those beautiful, bright, cloudless summer days, look for trout in the shadier portions of the stream.

Rain has varying effects on the fishing – it depends almost entirely on the atmospheric pressure. Rain itself is possibly beneficial: it may well improve the oxygen content of the water and consequently stir the fish into activity. If you like

133

fishing in the rain – some people do, I like it myself – and the approaching weather system is not a low, you may well enjoy very good sport.

The small stream will usually begin to colour quite quickly if the rain is prolonged. I have found that the start of such coloration has served me very well. The trout seem to sense that additional food is on its way into the stream and usually commence their feeding activities. Once the water is highly coloured, fishing the fly is not that effective – the little boys with their worms will have much better results. Extreme spate conditions usually bring on an extended feeding spell, and providing the water is not too coloured, good sport can be expected.

Very often when I have been fishing at dusk, and more particularly when I have been out shortly after dawn, I have met with that peculiar phenomenon when thick mist blankets the water. Usually this mist lies only inches deep while the air above is perfectly clear. Obviously this is caused by the sudden severe difference between the water and air temperatures. At times of dusk it has always created difficulties for me. Any hatch of flies seems to cease – or at least cannot be noted – and the fish seem to disappear suddenly. Whenever I have encountered this mist at dawn it has been a different story, the sport has been terrific. I cannot understand this difference, I state it here only for the reason that the observation may be of use to others.

I think that the effect of thunder-storms on trout are a mystery to us all. At times trout will feed avidly just before such a storm, or during a storm, or just afterwards. At other times it is the complete reverse. There does not appear to be any set pattern. Few anglers will want to fish during a thunder-storm, and it is probably dangerous to do so, but from time to time we are all caught out by such storms, when the fishing is completely unpredictable.

One such occasion happened to me in the Catskill

Mountains. I was staying at a fishing lodge that had been built on the banks of the Beaverkill River. The front porch and lawn were only a few yards from the water's edge and it was tempting to fish at odd times of the day and night. I had decided to do a little night fishing, and during the afternoon had mapped out several safe wading patterns. After a relaxed dinner I made my way across the lawn to the water. It had been a beautiful dusk and the night was clear and balmy. I commenced operations with a big, bushy, dry fly. I was unable to see it on the water but kept in sufficient contact to have a fair idea of what was happening to it.

After a short while I could see fellow anglers taking their after-dinner coffee on the covered porch of the lodge, which was very well lit. The light also helped me in my activities. Suddenly the sky lit up! Lightning and more lightning! Then the rain. No, not rain, a deluge! Within the space of a few minutes the lodge became just a glow through a sheet of water. I had on a loose fishing-jacket and hat, totally inadequate for what was taking place. I decided to quit as fast as I could. At that precise moment I had a solid rise to my fly, so definite that I felt a savage tug at the line. I had no alternative but to stand there in the deluge to play the fish out.

It was a beautiful brownie, about $1\frac{1}{2}$ lb (0.7 kg), and it fought very hard. The darkness and rain made it impossible to use a landing net, so I ended the tussle by scooping him up in my fishing-jacket! With the fish under my arm I made my way towards the lights of the lodge. I can just imagine the apparition I must have presented to those sitting on the porch! Do fish feed during a thunder-storm? Sometimes they do! However, the activity is not recommended.

Not all anglers can pick and choose the days they go fishing, and the weather must be accepted, whatever it may be, when the opportunity to fish comes along. The above notes may be of some help in indicating the quality of sport that may be expected. However, weather is a most peculiar thing, and the trout are not always predictable. If you have the chance to go fishing, then go, and take your chances. A day spent fishing is never a waste of time, even if you don't catch any fish. We learn something every time we are on the water, and it is that store of knowledge that brings future success.

AFTERWORD

It has been a great pleasure to have had the opportunity, in these pages, to fish with you and to discuss tactics and theories.

Our sport of flyfishing for trout is a demanding activity, not one that can be taken lightly as an occasional pastime. To obtain the full pleasure and satisfaction available to us we must constantly strive to improve our knowledge and technique. Many times we will be frustrated to the point of despair by the wily trout – but out of such frustration should grow a desire to overcome the difficulties.

Hardly any other activity could give us such an opportunity to be so close to nature. We are able to transport ourselves into the very environment of one of nature's most complex creations – the wild trout in its natural habitat.

The catching of the wild trout must be secondary to the pleasure obtained from outwitting him by accumulated knowledge. It is not necessary to kill trout to obtain this satisfaction. In fact, we should endeavour to conserve such a worthy adversary. The native wild brownie is a precious creature and future generations of anglers are entitled to inherit what we enjoy today.

By all means take the odd fish for the table, but not bags of fish just for the pleasure of showing them off to admiring friends or relatives. There is much satisfaction to be had from seeing them scoot away after release – at times I have almost believed that their tails wave a cheery farewell as they swim off.

I sincerely hope that at some time in the future we will meet on some stream and build on the friendship started here – perhaps even pursue 'wild brownies' together.

INDEX